Guidance on heritage assessment

"Our cultural diversity is what unites us"

Document prepared within the framework of
the Technical Co-operation and Consultancy Programme

Directorate of Culture and Cultural and Natural Heritage
Directorate General IV: Education, Culture and Heritage, Youth and Sport

Council of Europe Publishing

French edition:

Orientations pour l'évaluation du patrimoine

ISBN 92-871-5858-4

Editor: Gabriella Battaini-Dragoni

Coordination· Mikhaël de Thyse, Anna Trigona, Valérie-Sophie Bougerolle

Text: Dr. John Bold, Council of Europe Expert

Design: Council of Europe Graphic Design Workshop
Cover images and photos: Council of Europe

Council of Europe Publishing
F-67075 Strasbourg Cedex

ISBN 92-871-5825-8
© Council of Europe, September 2005
Printed at the Council of Europe

Contents

Foreword

The Council of Europe has carried out over 85 field projects within the framework of the "Technical Co-operation and Consultancy Programme related to the Integrated Conservation of the Cultural and Natural Heritage" since it was set up in 1973. These projects have highlighted the expectations of the Organisation's member states concerning guidelines or advice. It was therefore decided to launch a series of publications on guidance on heritage policy matters.

The first volume in the series, prepared in 2000 by the Legislative Support Task Force, offered *Guidance on the development of legislation and administration systems in the field of cultural heritage*. The second, produced in 2001 by the ad hoc Group on Inventory and Documentation, is devoted to *Guidance on inventory and documentation of the cultural heritage*. The third, produced in 2004 by the ad hoc "Lisbon Debate" on rehabilitation, is on *Guidance on Urban Rehabilitation*.

The present volume, entitled *Guidance on Heritage Assessment*, is the result of a joint initiative of the European Commission (Directorate General for Education and Culture) and the Council of Europe (Directorate for Culture and Cultural and Natural Heritage): "Integrated Rehabilitation Project Plan / Survey of the Architectural and Archaeological Heritage" (IRPP/SAAH). This is part of the Council of Europe's Regional Programme for Cultural and Natural Heritage in South East Europe, under the general heading of Technical Co-operation and Consultancy Programme.

Since 2003, the project has been directed towards the countries of South-East Europe. The project has relied heavily on gathering information according to agreed standards, in order to ensure that participating countries develop a common management tool facilitating the institutional capacity building process and European integration, mobilising existing resources on recognised priorities, presenting potential social and economic impact, and offering a joint presentation of the common European heritage of South East Europe.

Concepts and principles are therefore presented in this book in the form of methodological guidance. In this publication, the Programme's intention is to establish guidelines for integrated conservation and the sustainable use of the heritage. In this respect, it is helping to devise new European standards and to uphold the democratic principles promoted by the Council of Europe.

I would like to thank Dr. John Bold, Project Leader for the Integrated Rehabilitation Project Plan, who brought together the works completed since 2003. I would also like to thank the other experts who, through their involvement in the South East Europe project, directly contributed to the development of those guidelines, in particular Professor George Lavas, Mr. Daniel Drocourt who participated in the early stages of the project, and Professor Clairy Palyvou, Professor Giorgio Gianighian, Mr. David Johnson, Mr. Andreas Heymowski, Mr. Pedro Ponce de Leon, Mr. Alkis Prepis and Ms. Emma Carmichael who participated in the operational phase of the project. These thanks would not be complete without including the Project Co-ordinators in the participating countries who made use of the opportunities created by the project and directly participated in the elaboration of the methodology in ensuring that it responds to the real needs and challenges facing them in their countries, namely Ms. Arlinda Kondi Toci, Albania; Ms. Mirela Mulalić-Handan, Bosnia and Herzegovina; Ms. Dolya Mladenova Yordanova, Bulgaria; Mr. Bruno Diklic, Croatia; Ms. Corina Lucescu, Romania; Mr. Borislav Šurdić, Serbia and Montenegro (Serbia); Ms. Milena Filipovic representing Ms. Lidija Ljesar, Serbia and Montenegro (Montenegro); Mrs Juljia Trichkovska representing Mr. Jovan Ristov, "the former Yugoslav Republic of Macedonia" and Mr. Bujar Demjaha, Kosovo/UNMIK.

Finally, I would like to offer special thanks to Mr. Theodossios Mastrominas, Principal Administrator at the European Commission, for his direct contribution to launching such important co-operation in South East Europe and in his continuous confidence in the expertise and the know-how of the Council of Europe in this field.

Gabriella Battaini-Dragoni
Director General for Education, Culture and Heritage, Youth and Sport

1.0   Introduction

1.1   Principles

The cultural heritage is fundamental to the building of national and European identities which celebrate unity, respect diversity and bring people together to face the future, informed by perceptions of place and an understanding of the past.

Within the broadly defined cultural heritage, the tangible built heritage plays a fundamental role. It is capable of a wide range of definitions, but at the simplest level it is customarily understood to include archaeological sites, monuments, standing buildings and their fixtures and fittings, and ensembles, variously described. All of these tend to be studied and valued as historically, architecturally or artistically significant entities. Their protection might be seen as an end in itself, a statement by society of its belief in the values which the artefacts embody and exemplify. All European countries subscribe to the idea of analysing and protecting the material evidence of past human endeavours, however narrowly or broadly they might interpret the potential range of interest or significance. Such activity is fundamental in helping us to understand where as individuals we have come from, and how societies and their conditions have developed over centuries, subject to economic forces, shifts of faith, violent change and peaceful evolution.

This proper emphasis on the investigation and protection of the artefacts of the past carries with it the risk that identification and protective measures might be seen as finite processes with clearly determined ends, capable of being completed in order to satisfy stable, agreed objectives. Experience shows however that neither the processes nor the ends can be fixed, if at all, for long. Heritage identification evolves as interests change, new discoveries are made, previous judgements are challenged and modified. We also must acknowledge that neither architecture nor our response to it is fixed. Both built reality and our perceptions of it are conditioned by cultural and historical circumstances which change over time. For practical purposes however we do have to impose artificial limits on our activities if we are to proceed at all. So there is still the idea implicit in the inventorisation of the built heritage, that notwithstanding the need for re-evaluation and revision, certain aspects of the activity are capable of completion and might be laid to rest, for a generation at least.

A distinction should perhaps be drawn however between the philosophy and practice of heritage management, since the compartmentalisation of governmental, legislative and fiscal responsibilities supports this notion of the finite. Bodies dedicated to the identification and protection of the national heritage customarily devote their time to identification and protection as primary ends in themselves: that is their job. If however we take a wider, less departmentally compartmented view, we might propose a broader definition of the ends in view and consequently a broader understanding of the notion of the built heritage. In proposing the idea of the 'integrated heritage', the Council of Europe does not seek to undermine the activities of existing heritage bodies, but by underlining the wider importance of that heritage, wishes to introduce the idea of instrumentality in order to emphasise *a fortiori* the fundamental role in all societies of those organisations which are charged with the responsibility for the identification and protection of the artefacts of the past. In adding the idea of instrumentality to the notion of the built heritage, we move towards a less narrowly focused, more holistic view of the subject: the integrated heritage. We go beyond the basic idea of identifying and protecting as activities which have a value in themselves in order to situate the activity more firmly as an integral part of a democratic process which has as its means the participation of all members of society towards the end of improving the overall quality of life for all.

The built heritage underpins our notions of our own social evolution. Through its identification and protection we gain an enhanced understanding of our place in the world. In protecting and rehabilitating buildings we are not just preserving them as examples of historically or architecturally significant moments from the past; rather we are asserting their relevance to the continuum of contemporary and future life, and by so doing we are making statements of value not just about artefacts but about ourselves. We are viewing the built heritage not just as object but also as signifier. Seen in this perspective, the heritage becomes integral not just to physical and environmental protection and development, a position which is now increasingly well understood, but it also becomes fundamental to all aspects of planning or otherwise influencing the processes of social and political evolution within democratic societies, in which all members have a stake. So in proposing here the idea of the integrated heritage we are emphasising the role of the heritage as a social investment and a basic component in an evolutionary process which is fundamental to the continuity and promotion of peaceful and open democratic societies.

The Church of Shipska, Korca, Albania

1.2 Methodology

The guidance in this book derives from the Council of Europe and European Commission Integrated Rehabilitation Project Plan/Survey of the Architectural and Archaeological Heritage (IRPP/SAAH). The project has been directed towards the countries of South East Europe and its purpose, context, methodology and impact are described below. The project has relied heavily on the gathering of information according to agreed standards, on proformas, in order to ensure that all participants were compiling information in the same way. In the course of the compilation of the proformas, it became apparent that these presented a generic opportunity as well as providing a specific analytical tool for a particular situation. It is considered that the proformas might usefully be used as checklists for comparable assessments in other countries and other circumstances. They are therefore presented in this book as methodological guidance for others to use according to their own circumstances and needs.

Following a description of the overall project and its impact, the methodological elements are presented in the same sequence as the activities within the IRPP/SAAH. In each case a general discussion and commentary is followed by the proforma which has been used in the first three phases of the project: the Questionnaire for Heritage Assessment, the Prioritised Intervention Lists (PIL), and the Preliminary Technical Assessments (PTA) which correspond to the "Operational Phase".

The Operational Phase has been developed with the requirements of international donors in mind and the PTAs will provide sufficient information for donors to declare an initial interest, even though further detailed assessment will be required. These later Feasibility Studies, which represent the fourth phase in the project, are required in order to provide detailed, costed proposals for the rehabilitation of individual buildings and sites. A proforma for feasibility is not included as part of this publication since such studies are considered to be too specific to individual circumstances to be capable of generic treatment, varying according to building or site type, location, condition etc. Needs will also vary according to the requirements of potential donors and according to local or national practices and regulations. Within the PTA however, it is suggested that compilers should bear in mind the feasibility stage of the project so as to avoid later duplication of effort.

2.0 The Integrated Rehabilitation Project Plan / Survey of the Architectural and Archaeological Heritage

2.1 Principles

2.1.1 Identification and management of the heritage

The Council of Europe has identified the advancement of a European cultural identity, enriched by cultural diversity, as a major principle in its activities. This was the basis of the 'Declaration on Cultural Diversity' of December 2000, in which the Committee of Ministers called upon the member states 'to examine ways of sustaining and promoting cultural and linguistic diversity in the new global environment'. The identification, celebration, conservation and protection of the cultural heritage of all countries and territories is central to the process of developing mutual understanding and respect. Indeed, this has been a core belief of the Council of Europe for half a century, promoted through successive declarations, resolutions, conventions and recommendations, now gathered together for ease of reference in a single publication with an accompanying commentary and review of policies and practice, *European Cultural Heritage* (Volumes I and II, Strasbourg 2002).

More recently, the rich and diverse cultural, religious and humanistic heritage of Europe has been emphasised in the Warsaw Declaration (May 2005) in which the Heads of State and Government of the member states of the Council of Europe emphasised the common values of democracy, human rights and the rule of law. Of particular significance in the present context is the emphasis given in the Declaration to the creation of sustainable communities (article 3); to fostering European identity and unity, based on shared fundamental values, respect for our common heritage and cultural diversity, and to fostering political, inter-cultural and inter-religious dialogue (article 6).

Beyond issues of principle, practical applications and guidance on legislation in the field of cultural heritage and the documentation of that heritage have also been the subject of other recent publications by the Council of Europe: *Guidance on the development of legislation and administration systems in the field of cultural heritage* (Strasbourg 2000), *Guidance on inventory and documentation of the cultural heritage* (Strasbourg 2001) and *Guidance on Urban Rehabilitation* (Strasbourg 2004).

These publications provide the necessary background to current initiatives in the realm of heritage identification and protection which have been prompted by the developing situation in South East Europe. Although arising from a specific geographical and political context and presenting a constructive and continuing response to it, the Integrated Rehabilitation Project Plan/Survey of the Architectural and Archaeological Heritage (IRPP/SAAH), outlined below, offers the possibility of providing generic methodologies applicable in other situations and adaptable to other specific circumstances.

Bridge of Mehmed-Pasha Sokolovic, Visegrad, Bosnia and Herzegovina

2.1.2 Integrated Rehabilitation

The subject of rehabilitation has played a central part in the guidance and recommendations of the Council of Europe for almost half a century, appearing in two Resolutions in 1968 on the preservation and rehabilitation of groups and areas of buildings of historical or artistic interest (Resolutions (68)11 and (68)16), and in Resolutions adopted at successive Conferences of European Ministers (on the Preservation and Rehabilitation of the Cultural Heritage of Monuments and Sites, Brussels 1969; on the Architectural Heritage, Granada 1985; and on the Cultural Heritage, Valletta 1992, Helsinki 1996 and Portoroz 2001). The fundamental part played by rehabilitation in the context of integrated conservation, with its attendant social and financial implications, was emphasised in the Amsterdam Declaration, which was adopted at the Congress on the European Architectural Heritage in 1975. The *Guidance on Urban Rehabilitation* analyses the Council of Europe's reference texts, presenting the way in which the concept has developed since the 1960s and, informed by the experience of on-site activities, proposes a definition of what urban rehabilitation means in practice.

The IRPP/SAAH project is the most recent manifestation of the need for integrated conservation to enable revitalisation and rehabilitation programmes for historic buildings and sites which fulfil social purposes and the needs of modern life without compromising their historical or cultural integrity.

The project is conceived as a specific and tangible contribution to the development of democratic, peaceful and open societies in South East Europe, in which the active participation of all citizens is promoted irrespective of religion, language, gender or ethnicity. It is predicated on the belief that human beings and nations progress and flourish through celebrating what they hold in common; through positively respecting diversity, rather than through negatively exploiting differences. The project is characterised by the recognition of the contribution of the architectural and archaeological heritage to the promotion of mutual respect for the identities of all peoples and the encouragement of greater well-being and an improved quality of life. It begins moreover with the belief: 'these things we hold in common'.

The heritage of each country, territory, community and religion is part of the common heritage of all Europeans, for which there is a common responsibility. The integrated conservation of the architectural and archaeological heritage, within the constraints of sustainable development, two key and recurring themes within current European heritage strategies, is predicated on a comprehensive vision which encompasses physical, sociological, economic, cultural, ethnic and religious elements. It represents a responsibility held by all Europeans, to be discharged for the benefit of current and future generations. It contributes also to harmonisation and co-operation between countries and their integration within the European Union.

The concept of integrated conservation involves a cross-sectoral, multi-disciplinary approach to heritage management, seeing the heritage as a dynamic asset rather than as a potentially inconvenient and self-contained barrier to the inexorable advance of development and modernisation. Integrated conservation makes the cultural heritage one of the primary concerns of spatial planning, urban development and environmental studies. This is a concept which is closely allied with the principle of sustainable development. This may be defined as development which meets present needs without jeopardising the ability of future generations to meet their own needs, although these might not always be easy to predict.

These concepts are now being employed in a new political situation. Following the fall of the Berlin Wall and the opening-up of central and eastern Europe, there has been an opportunity to promote more widely the cultural and natural heritage as an asset. This asset may, through being shared by all Europeans, not only increase knowledge and recognition, but also promote social cohesion at national and local levels, and so contribute to conflict-prevention through the encouragement of mutual tolerance. This ambition underlines the positive political role of the heritage, which has too often in the past been a negative focus for political dissent, social discord, violence and destruction.

The IRPP/SAAH project has been devised with a clear understanding of this positive political dimension, together with an equally strong condemnation, expressed by the Council of Europe and the European Commission, of its negative and destructive opposite. Although this political perception informs the project, the immediate goals are tangible and focused towards the managed rehabilitation of monuments and sites, balancing the need to respect historical and architectural integrity while rehabilitating and providing appropriate new uses for buildings and sites, together with new possibilities for those who live there. The project has a strong social dimension to accompany its historical and architectural elements.

2.2 Project management

The project was launched in 2003 in conjunction with the relevant national and regional authorities in order to make a direct contribution to the institutional capacity-building process in the seven countries taking part in the regional programme: Albania, Bosnia and Herzegovina, Bulgaria, Croatia, Romania, Serbia and Montenegro (including Kosovo), and "the former Yugoslav Republic of Macedonia". The intention of the project was to evaluate the needs, priorities and technical requirements associated with significant buildings and sites, with a view to conservation, restoration, the appropriate rehabilitation of buildings and sites in their social and cultural context, and long-term sustainability. As an end result, the project offers approaches to project management which are designed to fulfil not only national and institutional needs for improved mechanisms, but are also intended to fulfil the requirements of potential public and private donors. It represents a stage in a process towards attracting partners and funding bodies in order to secure concrete investments and to ensure that donors will have confidence in the security of their financial commitment. It is not the intention of the project to impose but to provide methodological tools and mechanisms which will enable national institutions within these countries better to help themselves. National professionals will be enabled to harness existing skills and knowledge and direct them with some common purpose towards achievable goals.

The approach adopted within the Council of Europe's general programme of Technical Co-operation and Consultancy, and more specifically within this particular project, is informed by certain core principles:

– local development is a factor in democracy;
– there must be a symbiotic relationship between local and national initiatives which should be mutually informing and mutually sustaining;
– local territory is an expression of identity, since it is at the local level that human activity and participation begins;
– the heritage is not just a matter of major nationally significant monuments but includes smaller localities which reflect the history and aspirations of communities which have lived in them for generations;
– identity is fundamental to cultural continuity, its recognition being critical to the celebration of diversity and the promotion of mutual understanding.

The celebration of national, regional and local identity is demonstrably capable of being employed in a manner inimical to the development of just and tolerant societies, when the views and beliefs of the committed are forcibly imposed on the reluctant or less certain members, but it is a fundamental tenet of the European project that unless we work towards a shared identity, we shall prejudice the building of a common future with a balanced development protective of the community and its members.

Electrical Plant, Kokaliane, Bulgaria

15

2.2.1 General remarks

South East Europe is a designation chosen in acknowledgement that the more commonly used collective name, the Balkans, is too often regarded as a pejorative descriptor of the region, with associated connotations of nationalist, ethnic and religious division. Rather than being employed as an overloaded metaphor, it should be understood as a portmanteau term for a group of neighbouring countries which are characterised by a complex and shifting history, great diversity and an extraordinarily rich cultural heritage. Geographically in the south-east of Europe, this is a region whose development politically, philosophically and historically is central to the European idea. Often in the past the playground of the 'Great Powers', the Balkan countries once more are in a state of political, economic, social and procedural transition, dealing with new political frameworks and developing market economies. These changes are reflected very clearly in the domain of cultural heritage management which is faced with the challenge of identifying, preserving and making better known the material evidence surviving within this cradle of the oldest European cultures. This is a region rich in evidence of settlements which reveal continuous habitation from the Paleolithic and Neolithic eras, through Hellenistic, Roman, Byzantine and Ottoman periods, and onwards towards the modern era. This is a multi-ethnic region with a complex, shared heritage. The findings of the questionnaires confirm both the importance of that heritage and the complexity of the situation which is being faced by small numbers of dedicated professional staff.

2.2.2 Project methodology

The IRPP/SAAH is jointly managed by the Council of Europe and the European Commission. The Council of Europe is responsible for its practical implementation and follow-up, and it also provides the Secretariat. Each phase of the survey is carried out in association with international Project Leaders and Technical Assessment Experts. Within the individual, beneficiary countries, under the umbrella of the Interministerial Commission set up to manage the *Regional Programme for the Cultural and Natural Heritage in South East Europe*, national Programme Co-ordinators provide the political support for the national Project Co-ordinators. It is the Project Co-ordinators who, as experts in their field, are responsible for organising the various activities required by the project within each country, co-ordinating the work of colleagues and providing the consistent point of contact for the Secretariat.

The project methodology, described in detail below, is four-fold, moving from the general to the particular, from broad assessment of heritage identification and management strategies in each of the participating countries, to the detailed specific consideration of the feasibility and costs of restoring and rehabilitating individual buildings and sites.

Stage 1: Heritage Assessments. This initial stage involved the completion of a questionnaire on the heritage by national representatives in each country, which was followed by visits from international experts who then produced in association with the national representatives a report on the heritage situation: legislation, mechanisms, management etc.

Stage 2: Prioritised Intervention Lists. National experts in each country produced descriptive lists of 15-20 monuments and sites which they considered to be prime candidates for rehabilitation and restoration. These were intended to cover a wide range of building and monument types – churches, mosques, archaeological sites, houses, urban and rural buildings, and ensembles – and a broad range of potential levels of intervention and rehabilitation cost, from major expensive projects to the more modest. The criteria to be followed were concerned with significance, current condition and risk.

Stage 3: Preliminary Technical Assessments. National representatives in each country, advised by international experts are responsible for preliminary evaluation of the works and strategies required for the rehabilitation of buildings and sites, assessing likely risks and costs and proposing potential future uses.

Stage 4: Feasibility Studies. These very detailed studies which are necessary before restoration and rehabilitation works can be fully implemented, represent the final phase of the IRPP/SAAH project. The requirements of feasibility studies will be subject to many variable factors according to building and site type, situation, condition, available expertise, stages in funding provision, requirements of funding bodies, and so on. The requirements are less capable therefore of being encapsulated on a simple proforma, so they do not form part of this guidance book.

2.2.3 Assessment findings and summary of the lists

The questionnaires and the subsequent reports on the countries participating in the IRPP/SAAH project have revealed that all of them have institutions which are staffed by immensely dedicated professionals who have a determination to consolidate strengths and to improve institutional and national situations where necessary. The reports have celebrated the rich heritage of all the countries, but have also identified many common problems as well as opportunities, in the transition to new legislative frameworks, in evolving management structures, in funding works on the heritage and in ensuring adequate training in documentation, project management and craft techniques. The reports provide the basis for further analysis of specific topics, as well as providing a context for the consideration of individual sites and monuments at a later stage.

The various Prioritised Intervention Lists include a wide range of building and monument types of local, regional, national and international importance. They illustrate a coherent understanding of a Balkans heritage based on its diversity. Such diversity is characteristic of European identity as a whole and the acknowledgement and celebration of this diversity was fundamental to the compilation of the lists.

The overall list of 160 monuments is a small but very significant sample from the rich heritage of Balkans buildings and sites. It includes a range of types and a range of potential restoration projects and funding opportunities, including smaller houses and rural ensembles as well as major secular and religious monuments. The lists may be analysed in a number of ways in order to produce a number of different results, since many of the categories of typological classification overlap. It is clear however that enormous emphasis has been given to religious monuments and sites. 70 of these have been identified: churches, monasteries, mosques and hammams, synagogues, and associated residential buildings. Urban and vernacular houses, commercial buildings and ensembles represent the second largest broad category: 43 sites, of which 17 may be regarded as urban or rural ensembles. There are also 23 archaeological sites (2 of which are underwater); 18 fortresses and barracks; and only 6 industrial or infrastructural buildings or sites.

Many of these examples are of obvious architectural or historical importance, but some of them call into question the conservation philosophy which is being applied in the compilation, since they may be regarded as significant sites of memory, requiring wholesale reconstruction, rather than being tangible buildings capable of restoration, rehabilitation and re-use. Current conservation best practice suggests that the value of a ruin or a destroyed site is as a stimulus to reflection, and intervention should be limited to protection from further decay, although it has been acknowledged that all forms of intervention designed to delay the process of inevitable lingering dissolution do in themselves alter the monument.

The majority of the interventions proposed involve buildings or ensembles of manageable size and scope. A small number of the archaeological sites however cover such large areas of landscape that the feasibility of any future single project would be called into question. Proposals for such sites would perhaps be best subdivided into a number of small, self-contained projects to be carried out over an extended period of time.

The lists sought to identify the significance of the sites and the urgency of carrying out works. Of the 160 buildings and sites, 30 were considered to be of international importance, 110 of national importance, and 20 of regional importance. The great majority of these (120) were considered to be of high priority for intervention, and the remainder of medium priority.

Lubenice, Island of Cres, Croatia

2.2.4 Impact of the project

In the participating countries of South East Europe, the requested format was closely followed, with the addition of a photograph, and the results for each country have been published together with the heritage assessments. There is now, for the first time, a list of 160 monuments and sites which are representative of the Balkans heritage as a whole. The list has added value and resonance through being compiled by national experts in each country. This national commitment to the compilation gives it a weight and a focus which an imposed internationally compiled list would lack. The lists provide a snapshot of priorities within South East Europe, compiled from a very specific standpoint. These lists, together with the heritage assessments, have now been published for each country.

The involvement from the beginning of the project of relevant national and regional authorities in all of the countries involved has ensured that individual countries and institutions have been regarded, and regarded themselves, as stakeholders right from the start.

The project has been designed as a tool providing mechanisms to help the institutions in the countries to help themselves, with the long term aims of institutional capacity building, the attracting of donors and the sustainable rehabilitation of monuments and sites. The project provides many constructive opportunities for networking between institutions and between the countries themselves, enabling the sharing of ideas, strategies and professional expertise within and between countries which are characterised by considerable diversity as well as having a great deal in common.

The project has also enabled international experts to learn from the countries through visiting sites and in compiling assessment reports, and has enabled the members of the national institutions to gain an external perspective on their own management and structural mechanisms. The close working relationships between national and international experts should ensure a better mutual understanding of different perspectives and will in particular enable the countries to better formulate their bids for international funding.

Through the production of brochures, explaining the project and its various stages, designed for a general audience, the Council of Europe and the European Commission have demonstrated their commitment to supporting the national authorities in the dissemination of public information about the project process, aims and ambitions. Public support is fundamental to the overall endeavour, and this depends on the provision of clear and timely information.

An incidental result of the preparation of Prioritised Intervention Lists has been the recognition of its value as the basis for an inventory of buildings and sites which is not just historical and factual in emphasis, but enables comments on significance and includes notes on condition and the need for interventions. These additional comments are fundamental to the primary purpose of the lists which is to provide a starting point in the process of attracting funding for rehabilitation.

It is recognised that although this project is finite, it should represent the beginning of a number of continuing processes. These include the continuing assessment of priorities for intervention on buildings and sites; the continuing assessment of possibilities for rehabilitation and appropriate re-use of buildings; the ongoing improvement of management structures and practices; the continuation of networking and the development of negotiation skills; the development of new and productive relationships with national and international partners.

The impact also confirms the utility of the project and its various components as a generic model for assessment and prioritisation which might, *mutatis mutandis*, be employed in other countries and situations.

Through the preparation of Preliminary Technical Assessments, the national authorities are developing the project proposals which will attract supporters and donors both nationally and internationally in order to restore and rehabilitate buildings and sites which have suffered from a lack of investment in the past. More detailed feasibility studies with further technical and financial assessments will be required before comprehensive works can be carried out, but the PTAs represent a crucial stage in focusing attention and raising the profile both nationally and internationally of neglected parts of the built heritage of each of the participating countries.

3.0 Methodological guidelines

3.1 Heritage Assessments

3.1.1 Background

The first phase involves the making of a heritage assessment. This is compiled on the basis of an initial questionnaire completed by a national project co-ordinator, following wide consultation with national and regional institutions, as well as with all cultural, ethnic and religious communities. The questionnaire provides indicative, but not exhaustive, guidelines with a view to identifying the sources of information and partners and in order to gather preliminary material, to be used in the preparation of national assessment reports on the current status of the architectural and archaeological heritage.

The published assessment report is specific to each national situation, but each attempts to investigate the same broad subject areas in order to provide a common understanding of problems and opportunities in each country.

The topics addressed through the questionnaires and the reports are generic heritage management subjects. They pose questions which legitimately may be asked of any national heritage institution anywhere in Europe, regarding its philosophical framework, funding regime and working practices. As such they provide a useful checklist of questions on legislative and institutional arrangements for heritage identification, protection and enhancement; existing management machinery and tools; as well as the available professional, financial and documentary resources. They consider the general political and policy context, the role of heritage in society, and specific areas for future activities and partnerships.

Such a checklist could usefully provide a framework for investigation in other national circumstances, for example in cases where funding bodies or sponsors require assurances about the security of their potential financial investment or other support. It might also be employed in the service of that institutional self-analysis which is frequently necessary before improvements in practices can be proposed and implemented. Finally, it contributes to the further development and updating of a database on the current situation of heritage policies and legislation.

The Hammam of Gazi Mehmed Pasha, Prizren, Kosovo/UNMIK

3.1.2 The Questionnaire

The questionnaire is designed to encourage the expression of views, including possibly contradictory opinions, as well as to gather basic facts about the heritage and its management. It seeks to elicit views about the nature and quality of the architectural and archaeological heritage, and to identify those aspects or examples which are deemed within the countries to be the most important. It solicits informed, professional views on the strengths and weaknesses within heritage management and legislation in each country and invites the national compilers to suggest ways in which the situation described might be improved.

The questionnaire is wide-ranging and therefore it requires consultation at national and local institutional levels within the countries in order to be completed. This form of assessment has proved to be valuable not just for the recipient of the information, but also for the compilers themselves since the act of gathering and marshalling information necessarily involves communication and discussion with colleagues, establishing facts and seeking clarification, thereby making it into a learning experience. It is very easy, indeed normal, in day-to-day work to lose sight of the wider context in which that work is being carried out. The questionnaires enable the compilers to look beyond the limits of their own desks, to make contact with colleagues and to canvass opinions in order to provide very valuable national information. As a result of this exercise, duplication of activities or a lack of clarity in existing procedures might be identified, leading to a better rationalisation of heritage management.

3.1.3 Recommendations

The questionnaire headings are itemised in the questionnaire table of contents (see below 3.1.4). These cover the following broad subject areas:

Heritage, Legislation, Management, Partnerships, Documentation, Ethnicity and Community.

The comments which follow represent general conclusions gleaned from the questionnaires and the reports completed and published in South East European participating countries in the IRPP/SAAH project. They are expressed here as advisory remarks rather than as critical statements about individual situations. They may therefore be applicable to countries in other parts of Europe. For details on the specific situation in individual countries, the reader should refer to the individual volumes on each country published by the European Commission and the Council of Europe.

Heritage

- The understanding, protection and promotion of the heritage as a fundamental part of national life, depends for its success on the support of the general public, who must be educated and kept informed, and of the government, which must be encouraged and regularly reminded to ensure that the heritage and related issues remain high on its list of priorities.

- Education, public support and political engagement represent a necessary continuum in heritage protection. This may be reinforced through partnerships between departments of culture and departments of education; through publication and through the involvement of the mass media.

- The heritage should be recognised as an economically viable contributor to the national treasury, not simply through tourism but also through the well-attested good economic performance of rehabilitated and re-used historic buildings.

- Consideration of the implications for the heritage should be a fundamental requirement in questions of urban and spatial planning. The apparent tension between the protection of the heritage and necessary development should be subject to discussion and negotiation at the earliest planning stages.

- Protection of the built heritage does not stand alone; it should be regarded as an aspect of integrated protection which also includes cultural landscapes and the natural environment.

- The heritage requires a large body of trained, professional staff. It is tempting to try to do too much with too few, since existing dedicated professional staff tend to mask staff shortages by working an anti-social number of hours. Recruiting and training younger staff is an investment for the future. Training is needed in all fields but it may be noted here that there are particular specialist needs in documentation techniques, new technologies, project management skills, and craft and restoration skills.

- The heritage is not finite; its examples come right up to the present day and include industrial and rural sites and modern buildings as well as older buildings and sites of obvious significance. Through emphasising the importance of major monuments we risk losing sight of the wider urban and rural vernacular context, and its related ensembles.
- The growth of urbanisation represents a particular threat to the heritage, threatening the urban environment with unsympathetic development, and causing the rural environment to become depopulated, leaving buildings and sites unused, dilapidated and abandoned.

Legislation

- Heritage legislation has to serve a number of purposes; it is therefore tempting to make new laws which try to answer every potential eventuality. It is preferable to create simpler, short laws, with greater detail expressed on specific aspects in subsidiary laws.
- Laws should not just be punitive; they should also provide incentives on, for example, the benefits to owners of owning historic buildings.
- There are aspects of the law which should be punitive: particular attention should be paid to illegal demolition, unauthorised building, treasure-hunting and the robbing of archaeological sites.
- Since the law must be implemented by administrators who will often have to explain matters to the general public, it is important to ensure that there are adequate interpretations available in the form of guidance notes.
- The implementation of legislation often involves unexpected impediments and procedural delays. It is important to have an implementation strategy which will enable continuing protection of historic buildings and sites even if the law is not yet fully operational.
- The law should provide for categories of evaluation of monuments and sites; some monuments clearly are more important than others.

Management

- Heritage management is an ongoing and dynamic process, always capable of improvement through better management strategies and structures; refined laws and practices; increased and better-directed funding.
- A Strategic Plan for the management of the heritage is fundamental to the activity. This should define what is done, how it is done, by whom, for whom, and the intended results.
- A plan should enable the clarification of responsibilities between national, regional and local bodies. This clarification is vital if the management of the heritage is going to be understood by the public. It should be clear to owners of historic buildings how the decision making process for pro-

posed works is implemented. In determining such matters, the institutions themselves will develop clearer and more logical procedures.

– Clarification of procedures and responsibilities is also required between secular and religious institutions, to ensure that religious monuments do not fall into a management and procedural void.

– In determining the roles of responsible authorities, consideration should be given to possible divisions of responsibility between archaeology and architecture; between sites and archaeological finds; and between the immovable and the movable heritage. Whether responsibilities are divided or merged will depend on many national institutional and professional factors: how the responsibilities are divided is less important than ensuring clarity of explanation and implementation.

Partnerships

– Institutions have partnerships with other national and local bodies such as museums, universities, and increasingly with international academic bodies and funding foundations. It would be beneficial in the case of the latter especially to develop guidelines for engagement: a national register of which organisation is involved in which project; how it will be funded; how it will be approved and monitored, would be desirable. Even if money is provided by international donors, national institutions should still exercise their rights to control and oversee developments. A register and a procedure for carrying out analyses of the process (post-implementation reviews) would ensure that practices are refined and lessons learned.

– Project viability in internationally funded works of restoration and rehabilitation will be dependent in part upon the demonstration of a clear management structure. There should be continuity within the management team and a clear distinction drawn between responsibility and accountability.

– Maintenance and rehabilitation of historic buildings to appropriate standards is costly. There is often a need therefore for donors, but these may not just be the large foundations. If the national heritage is a shared responsibility, then owners themselves of historic buildings may be viewed as potential donors, and perhaps given tax or other incentives in order to properly maintain the buildings. In the case of development on potential archaeological sites, the developer may also be regarded as a potential partner, a donor who pays for investigation of the site as part of the price of development.

– Management must respond to new financial imperatives and strategies: training for managers is required in project planning and financial management, whether funding is from national and governmental official sources or from national or international funding agencies and donors.

Documentation

- The identification and protection of the heritage requires strategies. The creation of an inventory is fundamental but it is an activity which should be defined by a strategy; it does not in itself provide the strategic justification for heritage protection.

- The improvement in national approaches to documentation involves the adoption of agreed technical guidance in inventory, for example through the use of European Core Data Standards; the employment of agreed archival standards for the care of photographs and documents; and the employment of sufficient staff who must be trained in computerisation and collections management.

- Documentation of the architectural and archaeological heritage should, wherever possible, be made publicly accessible. It may be desirable when databases are created to provide different levels of access to the information so that confidential details of ownership or funding, for example, might be held and interrogated separately from the more general, publicly accessible historical information.

- Particular attention should be paid to the role of mapping in heritage identification, management and promotion. Maps may be linked to land registers in order to facilitate the identification of owners of buildings and sites.

- The documentation of the heritage should be regarded as a dynamic tool in its management, capable of being regularly updated as circumstances change and knowledge increases.

Ethnicity and Community

- The acknowledgement of the rights of ethnic groups and communities should go beyond the expression of passive respect for their heritage. Specialists from within ethnic groups should be positively encouraged and employed within heritage organisations in order to give informed advice on policies, procedures and significance.

- The need to acknowledge and protect the heritage of all ethnic groups and communities is a constant requirement in heritage education and management. Although cultural monuments may be identified according to ethnic, religious or community criteria, their protection is a common responsibility. The heritage is an expression of all the population in all its cultural diversity: diversity and commonality should both be celebrated. This must be underlined through training, education and promotion to the public.

– The heritage should be viewed as a manifestation of those qualities and attributes which we hold in common, rather than as a vehicle for the expression of difference and discord.

Archaeological site of Banja, Bansko, "the former Yugoslav Republic of Macedonia"

3.1.4 Questionnaire for the Assessment of the Architectural and Archaeological Heritage

Table of Contents

Introduction

Country or territory

1.0   Your organisation

2.0   Main characteristics of the heritage

3.0   Legislation

4.0   Management of the built heritage

5.0   Staff in the official organisations/institutions

6.0   National partner organisations and activities

7.0   International partner organisations and activities

8.0   Relationship between planning and heritage

9.0   Funding

10.0   Documentation

11.0   Prioritisation

12.0   Ethnicity and community

Introduction

This appendix document to the Terms of Reference of the Integrated Rehabilitation Project Plan / Survey of the Architectural and Archaeological heritage (IRPP/SAAH), jointly implemented by the European Commission and the Council of Europe within the programme framework, is addressed firstly to the IRPP/SAAH Project Co-ordinators appointed in countries participating in the *Regional Programme for Cultural and Natural Heritage in South East Europe.*

The questionnaire provides indicative, but not exhaustive, guidelines with a view to identifying the sources of information and partners and in order to gather preliminary material, which will be used to elaborate national assessment reports on the current status of the architectural and archaeological heritage. The preparation of these reports by the Project Co-ordinators (national) and the Project Leaders (international) is the first phase of the IRPP/SAAH.

The national assessment reports will present in a synthetic manner, the legal and institutional framework related to the protection and enhancement of heritage, the existing management mechanisms and tools, the resources available – both at the professional level (including budgetary concerns) as well as the documentary level. It will also take into consideration the political guidelines and the role attributed to heritage in society. It is on the basis of this report that the second phase of the IRPP/SAAH will elaborate the "Prioritised Intervention List".

Country or territory:

1.0 Your Organisation

Name of organisation:

Address:

Telephone number:

Function of organisation:

Contact name:

e-mail address:

2.0 Main Characteristics of the Heritage

What are the main characteristics of your architectural and archaeological heritage?

What do you regard as being the most important types of buildings?

What do you regard as being the most significant types of ensembles (e.g., monumental, territorial, urban/rural, infrastructural)?

Which aspects of the heritage do you regard as being most threatened?

What do you see as the main areas for intervention?

What are your current priorities for the heritage and its management?

What are the main strengths in the heritage management?

What are the main weaknesses in the heritage management?

What is the approximate number of single architectural monuments?

What are the main archaeological places?

What are the main architectural ensembles / the main traditional settlements / historical centres?

3.0 Legislation

What is the name and date of the current legislation pertaining to historic buildings and archaeological sites?

Is the legislation currently undergoing review and revision; if so, what is the target for completion?

Is this being done with assistance from the Council of Europe?

Does the current legislation offer definitions for specific areas of interest – e.g., definitions for monuments or sites; date range for these areas of interest?

What are the criteria for protective legislation of the built heritage – e.g., major monuments, religious buildings, ensembles, rural or industrial heritage?

In what language(s) is the written law available?

4.0 Management of the Built Heritage

Is there a stated policy for the management of the built heritage?

Is there a strategic plan for its future management?

What is the national (governmental) department responsible for the built heritage? What is the national (governmental) department responsible for the archaeological heritage?

Who are the authorities responsible for the religious heritage (protected or not)?

Describe the organisational (administrative) structure for the management of the built heritage at national, regional and local levels. Use an organisational diagram to show relationships between responsible organisations.

What is the working relationship between those departments, organisations or institutes responsible for heritage management, new building and town planning?

Comment on the divisions of responsibility between national, regional and local organisations.

How are the various organisations funded?

5.0 Staff in the official organisations/institutes

Comment on staff levels and expertise in the organisations, stating whether there are staff with high levels of regional or local knowledge.

Is there sufficient available staffing to embark on programmes of identification, assessment and prioritisation in all or some areas of the country or territory?

Will training be required before beginning the above; and if so, in what area(s) (e.g., identification or assessment of historic buildings; data base compilation; photography; project management)?

6.0 National partner organisations and activities

State whether there are partner organisations within the country or territory, with whom the built heritage institutions habitually work – e.g., Museum, University.

State the nature and frequency of the contact – e.g., regular transfer of data; periodic deposit of archaeological finds; occasional employment of architecture students, etc.

Are there any ongoing projects which are implemented with other partners in the field of built heritage? What are these projects? Have they been recently completed? Are they being developed? Have they been planned or proposed?

7.0 International partner organisations and activities

Is there an established mechanism for discussing/approving/assessing proposed works (architectural interventions, documentation, etc.) by international bodies?

State whether there are international funding bodies, NGOs etc., currently working in the country or territory.

State their programme and objectives and comment on whether the programme is being carried out with national agreement / approval / participation, or not.

Will any of the international programmes produce heritage documentation for a national, regional or local archive?

Are there any ongoing projects which are actually implemented with other partners in the field of built heritage? What are these projects? Have they been recently completed? Are they being developed? Have they been planned or proposed?

8.0 Relationship between planning and heritage

Is there a direct or indirect relationship between organisations of planning and organisations of protection?

Comment on how this relationship works – e.g. whether historic building experts have a role in town or country planning consultation and assessment procedures and in decision making.

Is there a problem with illegal construction; and if so, state the problem and what might be done to correct the situation.

9.0 Funding

In a climate of privatisation, how is work on rehabilitation and reconstruction of historic buildings being funded?

How much control or influence do the responsible organisations or institutes have in directing the funding and monitoring its success?

Are there differences in approach according to funding sources – i.e., are there different controls if the funding is national or international?

Is there an economic or taxation regime which offers financial incentives for sympathetic restoration of privately owned buildings?

10.0 Documentation

Which national, regional and local bodies maintain architectural and archaeological documentation: maps, drawings, reports, photographs, etc.?

Are the maps up to date; are there detailed cadastral holdings showing divisions of property; is it possible to link cadastral information with ownership information?

Is the documentation publicly available for consultation?

Is there a national inventory of buildings and sites; if so, what are the cri teria for inclusion – i.e. building types/dates?

What is the purpose of the inventory – i.e. is it an inventory which is solely for purposes of protection?

Does the inventory follow, wholly or partially, the Council of Europe Core Data Standard?

Does the inventory include characteristic 'ordinary' buildings as well as major monuments?

Does the inventory include ensembles (i.e. monumental, territorial, urban/rural, infrastructural) or is it solely a list of individual buildings or sites?

Is the compilation of the inventory an ongoing activity and if so, by whom?

Is the information indexed, and retrievable electronically?

11.0 Prioritisation

Would the task of prioritisation best be done by starting afresh, or could it be begun on the basis of existing material and expertise?

Is the inventory of sufficient sophistication to allow for initial considera-tion of priorities for intervention or is it mainly concerned with basic information on single major monuments or ensembles, without compar-ative judgements?

Are there people with local expertise from all communities and ethnici-ties who could advise on a programme of prioritisation?

What would you currently regard as the main areas or the main building types for prioritised intervention?

In prioritising work, balances will need to be struck between large numbers of competing imperatives – do you have the mechanisms in place for making informed comparative judgements on directing funding and expertise?

12.0 Ethnicity and community

What are the different cultural, religious and ethnic communities present in your country/region? Are there any official representative bodies for these cultural, religious and ethnic communities (name, address, etc.)?

What are the mechanisms by which people of all ethnicities and all communities may be involved in the programmes of identification, assessment and prioritisation?

Different ethnic groups may not necessarily recognise the significance of each others' buildings: how will you ensure that the interests of all groups are acknowledged and that prioritisation does not privilege the heritage of a numerically superior grouping to the detriment of smaller groups?

Are there problems (e.g., security) involved in exploring the built heritage of all communities; what strategies will be required to deal with them?

13.0 Training

At what stage and at what level do you consider that training will be needed in the following areas: documentation; assessment of the historical significance of historic buildings and sites; conservation assessment; craft skills; project management?

How would you like to see such training done – at institutes; in-house, with local or international instruction; abroad, on training visits?

Is there a crafts training institute, teaching traditional building skills?

14.0 Education

Do the official institutes and organisations responsible for historic buildings and sites have an educational role; are they involved with reaching the wider community through exhibitions, publications, explaining the significance of the historic environment in the media?

How could the responsible authorities gain wider public support through educational initiatives; how can they reach schoolchildren to help form the opinions of the next generation?

How will this proposed programme of identification and prioritised intervention be sold to the public; how will they be persuaded of its value and therefore give it their support?

15.0 Recording Programme

Do you have full access to the existing documentation?

Do you have staff trained in recording and documentation?

Is there expertise at local level which can supplement a national initiative?

Are there experts in particular building types who can be called upon to assist?

Are there representatives of different ethnic communities who can be involved in the programme?

Do you have access to planning information and expertise which could influence prioritisation of buildings and sites?

Do you have access to structural expertise enabling the assessment of damage and the costing of repairs?

Is there provision for entering the material onto a database?

Do you have adequate photographic equipment?

Who will hold the material once it is compiled?

16.0 Any Further Comments:

17.0 Bibliography:

Please indicate the list of documents consulted, copies or collection of documents, and the location (please provide the complete address) where these documents are kept and can be consulted.

Signed:

Date:

3.2 Prioritised Intervention Lists

3.2.1 Introduction

The architectural and archaeological heritage presents a subject area incomparably rich in content and capable of providing material for a wide range of analytical approaches. Both the subject and the potential approaches to it are as potentially infinite as any other area of intellectual enquiry. It is necessary therefore to impose limits if we wish to arrive at useful conclusions within a reasonable length of time. The process of compiling "Prioritised Intervention Lists" provides an opportunity to focus on specific aspects of the heritage, using limited criteria, in order to concentrate the minds of experts in their field towards achievable ends.

It is readily apparent that in countries where financial aid for monuments and sites has been limited, there has been an understandable tendency to accept the suggestions of international aid organisations and other donors if acceptance resulted in money being directed towards rehabilitation. Such acceptance however sometimes carries with it the possibility of a loss of national control over the disbursement of the financial aid, and a loss of choice in the decision-making process about where that aid might best be directed from the point of view of the national heritage as a whole. One of the purposes of the IRPP/SAAH project has been to help the national institutions to take a more pro-active role in identifying the heritage at risk and in soliciting financial aid for its rehabilitation, rather than allowing funding bodies to decide for themselves where aid might be directed.

Mileseva Monastery, Republic of Serbia, Serbia and Montenegro

3.2.2 Method

Following the questionnaire and the assessment report, each country's experts are invited to draw up their own "Prioritised Intervention List" according to three major criteria: Significance, Current Condition and Risk.

The purpose of the Prioritised Intervention List is to identify buildings and sites of significant heritage importance, which are considered to be in urgent need of conservation and/or restoration. This list should include examples of the whole range of buildings and sites with a significant heritage value. It should follow the broad principles of Council of Europe and European Commission policy in including examples of the religious heritage of all denominations; in considering ensembles as well as single monuments; in acknowledging the architectural and archaeological heritage as a continuum by considering the range of buildings, ensembles and sites from the earliest times to the present day; and in considering sites which have a local, regional and national value as well as those of obvious international significance.

In drawing up the list, experts in each country are involved in a continuing dialogue with colleagues, which is necessary from the beginning of the project, in order to ensure a degree of national consensus about the final lists. The compilers are invited to prepare lists of a limited number of buildings and sites (15-20 were proposed in each of the IRPP / SAAH participating countries), using the headings listed below. They are asked to consider the whole range of protected buildings and sites, rather than emphasising the importance of one type over another, in order to demonstrate that range and also to ensure that a range of funding options is likely to be required. This is not just an attempt to invite each country to list its most important and complex monuments which are likely to be the most expensive to restore. The lists are designed to cover a range of sites with an equivalent potential range of funding options.

The list should provide a snapshot of priorities, compiled from a very specific standpoint. It should describe significance and condition; the various threats faced, both internal – ownership, occupation and management, and external – exposure to environmental damage of natural or human origin. It should be based on the most reliable data currently available, but it is provisional. The lists should be compiled with the understanding that further detailed work of technical assessment will be required before funding options can seriously be explored. It is also understood that lists such as these are part of a continuing process of assessment, compilation, review and refinement. As buildings are rehabilitated, others in need will be identified. So the continuum of the heritage should be reflected in a continuity of endeavour regarding its preservation and rehabilitation. The need for funding will continue.

Since perceptions of significance and value are subject to change according to knowledge, enthusiasm, fashion and mere pragmatism, we might anticipate the desirability of further broadening the content of lists of this type. It is appropriate at a first stage that older sites which traditionally have been regarded as especially important should receive priority. In the future however some consideration should be given to twentieth-century buildings whose importance and quality might not be recognised until after they have been demolished.

The finalised Prioritised Intervention Lists demonstrate the broad utility of the list headings for eliciting sufficient information to enable the making of broad judgements about the heritage and its protection. They enable an initial assessment of significance and priority. Such assessments must be done by experienced professional staff with the appropriate high level of architectural or archaeological expertise which is required for statements of summary and judgements of relative value. The assessments will however require refinement before full evaluation of potential projects can take place, but as a mechanism for drawing up preliminary short-lists, the PIL headings may have a general application beyond their immediate purpose in the IRPP/SAAH project. It is suggested that the proforma below, which benefits from established practice elsewhere in borrowing some categories of evaluation, might usefully be employed as a checklist of points for consideration when attempting to prioritise heritage activities and funding in other countries or situations.

The headings and questions below are designed to assist the national authorities in drawing up and prioritising the lists. The finalised lists will then provide a starting point for a Preliminary Technical Assessment on the buildings and sites, involving further technical evaluation and cost estimates, prior to full feasibility studies.

3.2.3. Prioritised Intervention List for the Architectural and Archaeological Heritage form

1. Country, territory and organisational details:

Country or territory:

Name of organisation compiling the information:

Contact name:

email address:

2. The monument, site or ensemble:

Name and address of building(s) or site:

Inventory reference number(s) (if applicable):

Building/site type(s):

Main date(s):

Current use(s):

> *Notes 1-2. It is recommended that a photograph of the building or site is attached to the form next to the introductory organisational and identifying information.*

> *After the name, address and inventory number, brief descriptive statements should be made of type(s), date(s) and use(s):*

> *eg.i. Archaeological remains of Roman thermal baths; 3rd-6th century AD; in process of excavation.*

> *eg.ii. Public baths; 1563-4; partially in use for exhibitions.*

> *eg.iii. Orthodox church; 17th century; occasional (feast day) use for religious services.*

3. Description, and Assessment of Significance:

In all cases, consider here and state the structural and historical factual information. Then consider the archaeological, architectural, historical, social, cultural, religious and ethnic significance of the monument or site.

In the case of a monument or group of buildings, any special details of typology, construction, decoration, inscription and contents should be mentioned.

In the case of an archaeological site, give an idea of the number and type of monuments, a history of excavations, findings, deposit of findings etc.

In the case of an ensemble, its overall composition should be described (eg. mosque and hammam; group of farm or vernacular buildings; group of urban buildings with townscape value). State also whether it is monumental, territorial or infrastructural (for guidance on the classification of the ensemble, see the Council of Europe publication, Guidance on inventory and documentation of the cultural heritage, 2001).

4. Categories of Significance:

Consider here the Local, Regional, National or International significance. These may be listed as follows:

- *Internationally important*
- *Of outstanding national importance*
- *Of special national interest*

- *Of regional or local importance*

Notes 3-4. The description should be as simple as possible a statement of facts. It should be followed by an assessment of significance, which is one of the key elements of the exercise. Since judgements of significance are relative rather than absolute, they demand considerable professional knowledge of the site and its historic and typological context – the views of other experts may need to be canvassed.

eg. This is a basilican church with a simple tower. It is decorated with frescoes painted in 1650. The church is significant in testifying to the survival of the Orthodox Christian community in Albania after the Ottoman invasion.

5. Categories of ownership or interest:

State here the significance of the building or site in terms of religious denomination, ethnic grouping etc.

Note. This presents an opportunity further to qualify the remarks on significance by noting the importance of the building or site in the religious or ethnic context.

6. Documentation and bibliographic references:

State here the sources of information in inventories, archives, literature etc. State the extent of the archival information, eg. full photographic record, measured drawings etc.

Note. This is a summary statement of the extent of the documentation, and its location, together with a brief bibliography.

7. Condition:

This may be graded from very bad to good; state and describe the category of condition as follows:

1. *Very bad – structural failure and instability; loss of roof covering; major internal deterioration; major fire or disaster affecting most of the building.*

2. *Poor – deteriorating structure and/or leaking roof; outbreaks of rot; general internal deterioration; partly affected by fire or disaster.*

3. *Fair – Structurally sound but in need of minor repair and maintenance.*

4. *Good – Structurally sound; weathertight; no significant repairs needed.*

41

> State whether the building has suffered war or associated damage, grading the damage 0-5 as follows:
>
> 0. No damage
>
> 1. Small amount of damage sustained
>
> 2. Repairs needed to windows, doors etc., following damage
>
> 3. Up to 30% roof damage, but can be repaired
>
> 4. Roof more than 30% damage, with significant damage to walls, but can be repaired.
>
> 5. Destroyed (but may be a candidate for reconstruction)

8. Risk:

Risk is dependent on condition, ownership, occupation, management and natural hazards (eg.erosion, ground water, animal activity etc). All of these should be considered.

It may also be dependent on adverse demonstrations of identity, ethnicity or faith: state such potential risks if known.

9. Condition risk:

This may be graded A-H, as follows:

A. Immediate risk of further rapid deterioration or loss of fabric; no solution agreed

B. Immediate risk of further rapid deterioration or loss of fabric; solution agreed but not begun

C. Slow decay; no solution agreed

D. Slow decay; solution agreed but not begun

E. Under repair or in fair to good repair but no user identified or under threat of vacancy

F. Repair scheme in progress and end use and user identified

G. Building(s) in good condition but without use or user

H. Building(s) in good condition with use and user

Notes 7-9. The assessment of condition and risk are crucial in the overall assessment of the priority which should be given to the site. These categories of assessment are derived from the Buildings at Risk register compiled by English Heritage, extended here to include buildings in good condition. The war damage criteria are taken from the United Nations' categories of damage, extended to include buildings which have not been damaged at all. In certain cases the compiler *may wish to note the possibility of potential damage through adverse demonstrations of identity, ethnicity or religious faith.*

10. Technical assessment and costings:

State whether any technical assessments of condition have been carried out and whether there have been any preliminary costings carried out for repairs and rehabilitation. Specify and state the estimated costings if known.

Note. This is not the occasion to embark upon a new costings exercise – that will follow. Here it should be stated whether technical assessments and costings have already been conducted, stating the estimated costs, if known.

11. Ownership:

State whether private, governmental, municipal, religious, commercial, international, public utility or other. State if the ownership is unknown. State if the owner is known but absent.

12. Occupation:

State whether fully or partly occupied and whether in regular or occasional use.

13. Management:

Who is responsible for the management of the building – eg. the owners, the occupants, the users ?

If funding were to be made available, who would be responsible for administering the funds and overseeing the works ?

Notes 11-13. Ownership, occupation and management of the building or site are crucial in the assessment of condition and risk, and in planning the future strategy for the building or site.

14. Summary:

As an aid to prioritising, summarise the main points of Significance, Condition and Risk, using the grading as applicable.

Comment on the potential priority level of this building, ensemble or site: High, Medium or Low.

> *Note. The priority accorded to the building or site will be a matter of professional judgement, based on both intrinsic value and relative significance. Since this is ultimately a guide to future actions, it is important to avoid overstating the significance or priority level. If everything is considered to be as significant as everything else, it will be difficult to make the necessary decisions on priorities for further investigation and funding. An honest assessment will ultimately be the most useful.*
>
> Sign and date.

3.3 Preliminary Technical Assessments

3.3.1 Introduction

Following the heritage assessments and the Prioritised Intervention Lists, the preliminary technical assessments represent the third phase of the four-phase evaluation programme in the IRPP/SAAH. The fourth phase, detailed feasibility studies, falls outside the scope of this publication since such studies will vary enormously according to the type of monument and the complexity of the situation and the requirements. They are less capable therefore of allowing their key components to be encapsulated on a single, simple form.

The purpose of a preliminary technical assessment (PTA) is to identify technical requirements and broad cost estimates for each phase of every proposed intervention, from initial conservation to full rehabilitation, required at each building or site identified on the Prioritised Intervention Lists (PIL). Since the PTA follows the PIL, a certain amount of information relevant to technical assessment will already have been gathered. The guidance document which is published below was designed in order to ensure a consistency of approach across countries and across building and site types, presenting methodological guidelines for a technical activity. Since this phase of analysis is a crucial operational and programmatic stage in the process of attracting potential donors, it has been drawn-up with the requirements of international funding agencies in mind, acknowledging particularly the information requirements of the Council of Europe Development Bank and those of the World Monuments Fund (WMF). It may be noted here that the criteria for WMF funding fall broadly into three categories: the historic or artistic significance of the monument or site, with particular emphasis on its evolution; the degree of risk, or danger of deterioration; the viability of the proposed project.

Within the IRPP/SAAH project, the drawing up of PTAs is the responsibility of national experts, appointed by national authorities, supported by the

European Commission and the Council of Europe, and guided and overseen by international experts in order to ensure a consistency of approach across the region. Although different national experts may be required to advise on different sites according to their specialist expertise, the authorities should aim to establish a small core team of experts responsible for the preparation of the assessments, directed by a project leader. This should ensure a consistency of approach and provide the established point of contact which is necessary in long and potentially complex international communications and negotiations.

The PTA is a stage in a process, not an end in itself. It is a stage on the road to rehabilitation of the building or site, not an academic document which seeks to convey the results of primary investigation. Its purpose is to guide compilers in the gathering and assessment of as much information as possible within the constraints of time, expertise, access to the building or site, accessibility of documentation and availability of knowledge. It is recommended that no more than two days should be spent on site and no more than two days at the desk. The depth of the investigation should be conditioned therefore by available time rather than the desire to be comprehensive. The document cannot answer all questions: compilers should attempt broad scale rather than exhaustive detail, and they should keep open the possibilities for the future of the monument or site. Further works of assessment or of physical restoration will themselves prompt refinements or even radical changes in views about future uses of buildings: it is important to keep open options for future uses for as long as possible. It is also important to note the desirability of subdividing any proposed project into finite phases – repair the roof, for example, before worrying about long-term use.

If it is decided that the subject of the PTA requires full restoration or rehabilitation, it will then require a much more detailed Feasibility Study. It is a fundamental purpose of the PTA to enable the gathering and analysis of information which will lead to an informed decision about the need for such a subsequent detailed study. Compilers should avoid attempting to make final recommendations for the re-use of buildings at this stage; they may wish to make suggestions, but the more detailed findings of Feasibility Studies are required before the complete cost estimates, phasing of work and recommended uses can be finalised. However, although preliminary, the budgetary implications of suggested works should be addressed here in order to give a broad overview of potential costs which will be refined at a later stage. It is likely that the detailed work on the Feasibility Studies will prompt further ideas for future uses, so it is important to keep options open for as long as possible.

The PTA form is divided into three sections which are sufficiently broad and generic to allow the compiler(s) to make assessments and evaluations of buildings and sites of all types, while providing the levels of detail appropriate for technical assessments and initial costings. The three sections are as follows:

Sections 1-5: an introductory statement of the significance of the monument, the opportunity offered by funding, and the preliminary overall intentions for its future management; followed by a brief digest of the information gathered for the PIL: administrative responsibility, legal status, condition, documentation, projects planned or in process.

Sections 6-9: the detailed assessment enabling an evaluation of the historical or heritage significance of the monument or site; an assessment of its vulnerability; a technical assessment of the potential types and phases of intervention; a summary of the vision for the site and its sustainability; a preliminary assessment of costings; initial recommendations for the future of the site and its management; preliminary recommendations for the subsequent feasibility study.

Appendices: these provide checklists for technical descriptions and indicative threats; these are generic lists which are not specific to a particular building type or national situation, so they provide a starting point for the compiler(s) who may wish to develop their own type-specific or national checklists.

Particular attention should be paid to the elements which are likely to be required by donors in evaluations of funding potential: the Executive Summary (2); the summary statement of significance (7.2.1); the vulnerability/risk assessment (7.3); the summary of the vision for the site and its sustainability (7.6.1). It is particularly advised, throughout the process of compilation of information, to maintain a close view of the intended target audience of the assessment, so as to avoid later, time-consuming duplication of activity, going over the same things twice.

Summaries of significance and the vision for the site will necessarily be the major statements which will serve to attract the political, economic and public backing which is vital for the support of a successful and sustainable project.

3.3.2 Preliminary technical assessment form

1. **Introductory page**

   At the top of the page state the simple, identifying title of the building or site:

   eg. i. Electrical Plant, Kokaliane

   eg. ii. Husamedin-Pasha Mosque

   eg.iii. Church of Shipska

   Include a photograph of the building or site together with an extract from the map showing its location.

   List the following organisational and monument details:

   1.1 Country or Territory:

   1.2 Name of organisation compiling the information:

   1.3 Contact name:

   1.4 Email address:

   1.5 Name and address of building or site:

   1.6 Inventory reference number(s):

   1.7 Building/Monument/Site type:

   1.8 Main dates:

   1.9 Current use(s):

2. **Executive Summary: the site and its management**

   This is a summary statement of the significance of the monument or site, the risk or danger to which it is subject, the opportunity which will be offered by funding, and the preliminary overall intentions for the future management of the monument or site. It is a summation of the significant points about the monument or site and your preliminary proposals for its future. The summary should take into account some of the pre-requisites for grant aid: policy background; degree of sustainability; institutional capacity – support, management and participation.

   The summary must be brief and to the point so that it can be quoted directly to government ministers and potential funding bodies as an encapsulation of the situation and proposal, bearing in mind that many readers of this document will read only this paragraph. Politicians and funding bodies require short, cogent summaries which will help to convince them of the importance of the subject and the relevance of the proposals.

This executive summary should be written last after all the other information and conclusions upon which it depends have been gathered. It should not exceed 500 words in length.

3. Administrative information

3.1 Responsible Authorities

State here the relevant national, regional or local authorities with statutory or managerial responsibility for the monument.

3.2 Building/Site, Name and Address

Give full details of name and location, stating as applicable the address and the region.

3.3 Map reference

State the spatial referencing system in use, and the X and Y co-ordinates.

3.4 Type of monument

Architectural, Archaeological, Ensemble etc., specifying house, church, mosque, tombs etc. State whether Urban or Rural. Indicate here if there is a combination of architectural and archaeological features.

3.5 Ownership

This should include a statement of ownership, occupation, current use, as relevant.

3.6 Statutory Protection/Constraints

State here the level/grade of statutory protection and the statutory constraints, i.e. the limitations on possible actions, the need for official permission for works, etc.

4. Summary of condition

This repeats some elements of the PIL, although the more detailed work on the PTA may prompt a revision of the initial assessment.

4.1 Summary of Physical Condition – very bad to good

4.2 Condition Risk Assessment – graded A-H

4.3 Priority for intervention – High/Medium/Low

5. Existing information

5.1 Documentary sources:

Reports, drawings, photography (aerial and terrestrial), photogrammetry, video, publications etc. Comment on their existence, their location, their availability, their applicability and their quality.

5.2 Bibliography:

Comment briefly on the availability of published information, listing the main sources. Include internet references.

5.3 Fieldwork already conducted:

State here the technical assessments of restoration/rehabilitation etc. which have already been completed. Give the date and the recommendations which were made at that time.

5.4 Projects in progress:

State whether there are any projects in process on the building or site. State their scope and state who is responsible for the work.

5.5 Projects already planned:

State whether there are any projects planned for the building or site. State the proposed scope and who will be responsible for the work.

5.6 Financial estimates already made:

If estimates have already been made, give dates and details for categories of work; state whether the estimates have been presented as timed and costed phases, eg. i. secure the roof; ii. replace doors and windows; iii. convert to new use. Works to be considered in this section may include engineering and technical works; conservation and restoration works; adaptation; related public services or infrastructure, etc.

6. Scope of the PTA

6.1 Extent/Nature of the assessment:

State the numbers of people involved, their specific expertise, whether national or international experts, the length of time spent on the task.

6.2 Limitations of the study:

Give details for example of difficulties of access for reasons of ownership, occupation or dangerous structure; lack of available documentation; difficulty in consulting documentation; indicate time constraints on the study, if any.

7. The PTA

Here there may be repetition and expansion of some of the findings of the PIL. It is important to note that 7.1 (Background) is descriptive and objective, whereas 7.2 (Significance) may be more subjective in encouraging the introduction of judgements of relative value.

7.1 Background: Form, Function and Evolution

7.1.1 Summary description of the building/site, with comments on its urban or rural context if appropriate.

eg. A hydro-electric power plant in a rural setting close to the village of Kokaliane, a short distance from Sofia. The plant comprises a machinery hall with surviving Belgian electrical equipment, together with associated administrative and accommodation buildings.

7.1.2 Summary historic development and evolution of the building or site, from the earliest times until the present day.

eg. The plant was built in 1900 by Italian experts. It functioned until 1972. The buildings are structurally sound but in need of repair and rehabilitation.

7.2 Significance

In the assessment of significance it may be necessary to distinguish between the significance of the building or site for heritage management professionals and its significance as a building or site for the community. For example, a building which has been considerably altered from its original appearance, losing much of its historic or architectural specificity, may still carry great significance for its users, as for example, a site of memory – this should be acknowledged here.

7.2.1 Summary statement of significance/historical and heritage importance.

It is very important to draw attention here to the historical, archaeological, architectural, artistic, scientific significance of the monument or site, as applicable, using the checklist of possible categories, below. Mention any important association with historic and/or cultural events.

7.2.2 Checklist of categories which may be considered in the evaluation:

Historical;

Artistic/Aesthetic;

Technological;

Religious/Spiritual;

Symbolic/Identity;

Scientific/Research;

Social/Civic;

Natural;

Economic.

Note also the category of significance: International, National, Regional or Local.

eg. The plant is historically and technologically significant as the first electrical plant to be constructed in the Balkan region and is moreover a good example of the benefits of international collaboration, involving Italian and Belgian expertise. It is particularly noteworthy in retaining its original machinery in situ. As a result, the plant is considered to be of outstanding national significance.

7.3 Vulnerability/Risk assessment.

State fully the issues which have affected the condition of the site in the past. State the current problems of vulnerability or risk. Attempt to predict the potential future problems which will need to be addressed in order to ensure the appropriate continuity of the building or site. The issues may be natural, physical, developmental, concerning inappropriate interventions, lack of care from owners, administrative and financial weaknesses, etc. The main points should be summarised here, using the checklist of indicative threats in Appendix 2.

7.4 Technical condition

Summarise here the physical situation, bearing in mind that a far more detailed assessment will be required in the event of a feasibility study.

Assess levels and types of appropriate intervention: what could be conserved; what must be conserved; what could be changed (eg. intrusive later additions). Comment on the possible phasing of the proposed work, distinguishing between immediate stabilisation measures and longer term future interventions.

The technical description of the components of the building or site should be given utilising the checklists given in Appendix 1A and 1B, as relevant. For a site which contains both architectural and archaeological components, you may wish to utilise headings from both of the appendices. This technical description will be further developed in the event of a feasibility study.

7.5 Outline summary of required repairs

This is a preliminary, summary assessment, based on the findings of the assessment of technical condition. It will be the subject of greater refinement in the event of a feasibility study, but if some consideration is given to it here, it will act as a guide to those carrying out the more detailed, later work. Comment on the priorities and the possible phasing of the repair programme, drawing particular attention to works which should be carried out urgently to stabilise or secure the monument or site.

Note that 7.4 and 7.5 might be itemised separately and consecutively, or they might be combined if the monument lends itself to a unified assessment of condition and repairs (see the example in Chapter 5.3 below).

7.6 Conservation/rehabilitation policy and proposals

This should represent a broad statement of intention rather than a final manifesto for the building or site. It is a starting point, giving initial ideas, to be tested and elaborated at feasibility study stage. The following headings should be considered, and information provided as appropriate: fill in only those parts which are relevant.

7.6.1 Broad summary of the vision for the site, and its sustainability, at this preliminary stage.

Here there should be a consideration of the sustainability of the project and the proposed development. It should include a statement of intention and expectation of how the building or site will be managed in the future in order to ensure its long-term continuity and viability.

7.6.2 Conservation philosophy

Summarise purpose, scope, intentions; describe the authenticity of the structure, the appropriateness of the materials. Remember that the aim of this project is rehabilitation in the service of sustainable appropriate development.

7.6.3 Level of intervention

State whether the preliminary intention is to conserve as found; to repair, reconstruct or add to enable beneficial re-use; wholly to reconstruct as a monument of national significance, etc. If reconstruction is proposed, give precise reasons for the recommendation since such proposals are likely to be controversial and do not accord with conservation best practice which emphasises the protection from further decay of sites of memory rather than their reconstruction.

7.6.4 Preliminary proposals for appropriate uses, as applicable

eg. commercial, residential, community use, to be further tested at feasibility stage. It is generally considered that the best use for a restored building is a reversion to its original function, a church for example being best restored as a church, and a mosque as a mosque. However, since this is not always possible in all cases, alternatives may be considered and an appropriate but different new use may represent the best option. A change of function for example from a redundant electrical power plant to a museum of industry might well be appropriate provided that the conversion respected the integrity of the original building, retaining enough of its structure and character to inform and enhance the new, related function.

7.6.5 Opportunities for social uses and sustainable development

eg. creation of work places, engagement in social services, promotion in association with other activities such as tourism, commerce, information, museum activities etc.

7.6.6 Broad assessment of priorities for consolidation/covering, repair, conservation, restoration, rehabilitation

Divide these into discrete stages if desirable.

7.6.7 Public access

Wholly or partly, by arrangement; potential community benefit.

7.6.8 Other benefits

eg. engagement of a wider audience; features capable of particular exploitation

7.7 Finance

It is recognised that the detailed costings for a monument or site will not be achieved until feasibility study stage. It is also clear that even at that later stage, costings will vary according to levels of intervention, phases of work, choices for future uses of the building (where appropriate). It is however desirable to offer broad estimates of cost here, according to the best available knowledge, in order to offer a relative measure of the scale of the proposed project.

7.7.1 Broad assessment of budgetary needs and phasing;

This is not binding and is to be more fully assessed at feasibility stage. If immediate works are needed to secure the building or protect the site, highlight the costs of the necessary measures here.

7.7.2 Assessment of possibilities for attracting investments.

State here the nature of any objective financial estimates or projections which have been made, giving references to any supporting documentation.

7.7.3 Assessment of possibilities for recovering investments.

State here the nature of any objective financial estimates or projections which have been made, giving references to any supporting documentation. This may include scientific assessment of potential tourism but may include also other assessment of potential benefits to business or the local economy.

7.7.4 Have you already tried to raise funds for this site or monument? If so, provide details.

7.7.5 Have you already received funds for this site or monument? If so, provide details.

7.8. Management

Describe here the long-term and short-term arrangements for the management of any project for the building or site. Comment on any training needs which you have identified to ensure appropriate management practices and the long-term continuing viability of the building or site.

- *Institutional arrangements and responsibilities – national and local.*

- *Institutional philosophy – commitment to sustainability, access etc.*

- *Managing the process – who is accountable, who is responsible, who carries it out.*

- *Project board – composition and responsibilities, if applicable.*

- *Proposals for the long term management of the monument or site to ensure sustainability.*

Consider any preconditions, opportunities or constraints which are relevant to the sustainable development.

8. Documentation

It is recommended that the PTA is supported by photographs, drawings and a location map to supplement the written information. The photographs should illustrate the general points rather than attempting to cover all the detail, and may be limited to 6-10, although this may vary according to the complexity of the monument or site. The drawings also should be explanatory rather than comprehensive. Although detailed measured drawings will be needed for subsequent phases of work, at this stage sketches, or copies of archive drawings, will suffice.

9. Feasibility studies

These represent the next stage of the assessment process, but should be borne in mind during the compilation of the PTA. They will vary according to the type of monument or site. They are likely however to include the following: general statement; technical assessment; financial assessment; specialist assessments from quantity surveyors, structural engineers etc; existing fabric and condition; structural and service requirements; health and safety issues; design (and drawing) proposals; function recommendations; responsible authorities; outline of works – levels and phasing of intervention and associated costs; detailed account of beneficiary institution and management of the investment; next steps.

In concluding work on the PTA, recommendations on the content of a feasibility study should be considered, as an aid to the preparation of a brief for the next phase of work. Attention might be given to the following potential needs:

- further survey and analysis of structure to refine timing and costing of phases of work
- the need for particular specialist advice from structural engineers, environmental impact assessors, wall paintings experts etc.
- the need to consider the wider context of the building or site and its relationship to the environment.
- the need for equipment such as scaffolding.
- the need for further or improved documentation.
- the site management requirements.
- the need for a conservation plan for the building or site.
- the anticipated timing and costing of a feasibility assessment; bearing in mind that the costs may be borne by a potential donor, it is important to arrive at an estimated figure here.

PTA carried out by:

sign and date

Appendices checklists: Technical checklist and Indicative checklist of threats

The following appendices present checklists for the technical descriptions of the main aspects of the buildings or sites, together with a checklist of indicative threats. Use these lists as guidelines in this preliminary analysis: they are advisory rather than mandatory. Do not attempt to be exhaustive at this stage. The emphasis should be on scale rather than detail since there will not be time for a full analysis of all the relevant components. A more detailed analysis will be expected in any subsequent feasibility study.

Some sites will include both archaeological and architectural components so the compiler will need to refer to both checklists. These checklists of technical elements are generic rather than specific to a particular building type or national situation. Different types of buildings or sites may require the consideration of further, more specific elements. You are encouraged to develop your own type-specific descriptive checklists in due course, based on these guidelines, as the need arises.

Appendix I: Technical checklist

A. Buildings and Ensembles

The following components may be considered:

1. The overall structure (summary)
2. Foundations
3. Walls / Supports
4. Floors and ceilings
5. Roofs
6. Staircases
7. Doors and Windows
8. Balconies and Verandas
9. Wall Plasters
10. Decoration
11. Infrastructure
12. Auxiliary Structures
13. Out-door space / courtyards

In assessing components, the following may be considered, as relevant:

a. Description / constraints
b. Damage Assessment * (effects) / Threats **
c. Diagnosis * (causes) / Rate of deterioration
d. Proposed type of intervention
e. Priority of intervention
f. Estimated cost

* Damage Assessment and Diagnosis may be presented together

** For Threats see the indicative check-list in Appendix 2.

B. Archaeological Sites

The following components may be considered:

1. Broader Region / Environment
   Urban / non urban (in antiquity / modern)
   Landscape Values (in antiquity / modern)
   Accessibility (in antiquity / modern)
   Other points of interest in the vicinity (natural, cultural)
   Protective Zoning

2. Site

 Boundaries, fencing, security

 Accessibility, circulation within the site (access for people with disabilities)

 Excavated area (%), state of in-between areas

 Indications of unexcavated monuments

 Shelters

3. Monuments

4. Public Facilities / Site Presentation

 Public Access, car park

 Visitors' centre and facilities

 Exhibition and Educational areas, Museum

 Circulation (routes, paths, observation areas)

 Signage, Site interpretation

 Administrative facilities

 Infrastructure

In assessing components, the following may be considered, as relevant:

 a. Description / constraints

 b. Damage Assessment * (effects) / Threats **

 c. Diagnosis * (causes) / Rate of deterioration

 d. Proposed type of intervention

 e. Priority of intervention

 f. Estimated cost

* Damage Assessment and Diagnosis may be presented together

** For Threats see the indicative check-list in Appendix 2

Appendix 2: Indicative checklist of threats

Use this checklist to identify those threats which apply in individual cases.

1. Natural Threats

 Extreme natural phenomena (earthquake, tornadoes, volcanic eruptions)

 Natural phenomena triggered by human misuse (e.g. flood, fire, landslide, pollution)

 Erosion

 Pests, bird nesting, animal activity

Climatic factors (wind, rain)

Groundwater management (humidity migration, ponding, capillary flows of water, high or low water tables)

Solar radiation as an agent of deterioration

Thermal Fluctuations (expansion/contraction, wetting/drying cycles, migration and crystallization of salts)

Pollution

Decay of materials

2. Development – demographic growth

Urban spread

Agriculture (land use, mechanization, salinization of soils due to fertilizers)

Industrial Development, Infrastructure

Abandonment of countryside due to urbanization

Loss of handicraft tradition

3. Tourism

Lack of signage, clear paths, guarding, maintenance

Encroachment on sites of visitor facilities (and hotels)

Vandalism (e.g. graffiti)

Intensive visiting or usage

4. Lack of planning measures

Isolated 'digs'

Sites treated as 'obstacles to development' – garbage dumps

Provisionally fenced (to save the remains or to protect from the public)

5. The Impact of Social Unrest

Vandalism for political or social reasons

Destruction of symbols

Sites used for military purposes

Conflict of values

Staff of antiquity departments not trained for emergency actions

6. Looting

Demand in international antique markets

Poverty of rural areas – organized crime

Archaeology perceived as a foreign import

Treasure hunting

Failure to protect sites

7. Archaeological excavation as a damaging factor

Digs and trenches left open (no back-fill)

Consolidation, conservation and protection (and site presentation) not taken into consideration

Lack of coordination between scientific mission and local authority

8. Inappropriate Interventions as a damaging factor

Untrained personnel

Outdated methodology

Incompatible materials

Undocumented reconstruction disguised as restoration

Irreversible and ethically incorrect reconstructions

9. Lack of maintenance

Vegetation growth

Accumulated dirt

Stagnating water

10. Lack of administration and legislation

Inadequate institutional support

Unclear definition of the status of archaeological remains on private property

Vague criteria for designating protection zones

Poor integration of heritage into development plans

Inadequate training

Consciousness raising

Emergency plans

11. Structural destabilization

Structural failure – deformations, collapse

Loss of material, detachment, cracking

Additive effects -surface deposits, additions, replacements

12. Ownership and occupation
    Absentee owner
    Multi-occupation
    No responsibility for maintenance

13. Function
    Inappropriate function
    Conflicting uses

14. Resources
    Lack of finance for maintenance and repair
    Lack of skills for project management
    Lack of technical restoration skills

4.0 Conclusion

The basic principles and the main ideas underpinning the IRPP/SAAH project were not fundamentally new for the South East European countries. Most countries had inherited rich documentation accompanied by a system of protection from the previous communist regime which had proved to be quite efficient. Several countries subsequently had undertaken reforms and updated their systems, adapting their inventory systems according to European standards.

However, despite the professionalism and the convictions demonstrated in those reforms and in the development of good documentation systems, it is not betraying partners in the participating countries in the project to note that, in a few cases, the existing working methods do not always function effectively in fulfilling the requirements of the management and conservation of the integrated heritage. Much work remains to be done in order to integrate heritage concerns and the needs for protection and rehabilitation into the global strategies of development and reconstruction. The complementary components proposed as part of the Regional Programme for *Cultural and Natural Heritage in South East Europe* are set-up to help the countries improve their management systems and practices in accordance with the experience they have received from the IRPP/SAAH project and the problems which might have appeared throughout the implementation process.

The implementation of the project has presented new dimensions and challenges which are being successfully negotiated in these countries. The notion of priority and its promotion as a dynamic tool capable of mobilising resources and attention was initially difficult to translate into established practice, since it involves a strategic approach in which projects are spread over a long period of time, organised in short-term, intermediate and long-term phases. The need to develop a professional and political network was easier to understand since the south-eastern countries have learnt from their recent painful common history, that there is no better way for them to play their role in Europe than through the promotion of their common heritage. This involves collaboration between the countries as well as networking within the countries themselves, but this tends to go beyond the administrative limits of the individual institutions which have finite tasks and goals. It implies transparency, sharing of information, discussion and consultation in order to achieve consensus, this being a pre-requisite in presenting a clear and robust position to those who have to make the decision to support or to invest. International networking is also a challenge in itself, but easier to implement in view of the great willingness of all Central and Eastern European countries to open themselves to the world after decades of isolation: this enthusiasm for greater international co-operation makes them more receptive to the opportunities offered by globalisation.

Through this project, a very specific and pragmatic approach has been defined in South-East Europe in order to adapt European standards and good practice to the needs expressed by the South-Eastern countries themselves. National experts have developed a mechanism which respects local and national traditions and the high levels of existing skills, while acknowledging the legal and institutional expectations of potential international partners. An original and effective methodology has been achieved, as demonstrated by the results.

When finalising this book, the operational process of the project was still in progress and expectations were directed towards the institutionalisation of the working method in order to make its use sustainable and of continuing utility within the countries. The initial impacts, so far recorded, offer scope for optimism in pursuing this objective:

– in Albania and in the Kosovo region, authorities have redirected the available budget in favour of monuments studied during the project.

– in Montenegro, the method has been adapted as an initial step in carrying out an emergency inventory of more than 350 monuments which did not benefit from proper documentation.

– the dossier compiled for the Prioritised Intervention List was successfully exploited by Bosnia and Herzegovina in submitting a dossier to the World Monuments Fund for inscription of the 16th century Mehmed-Pasha Bridge over the River Drina on the list of "100 most endangered Monuments".

– Croatia was the first country to use the documents they produced as part of the project to apply for a loan to the Council of Europe Development Bank, obtaining 30 million euros for rehabilitation in Vukovar.

– In the Kosovo region, the Prioritised Intervention List contributed to the preparation of the working document presented to the Donors Conference organised by UNESCO in close co-operation with the Council of Europe and the European Commission. Moreover, the Preliminary Technical Assessments have directly contributed to the implementation of restoration and protection action for the Orthodox monuments damaged during the violence of March 2004. Technical reports were used by the Implementing Committee for the Restoration of Religious Buildings chaired by the Council of Europe.

All these examples of concrete exploitation of the methodology elaborated within the project suggest a progressive integration of the procedures and the logic into the daily practices of professionals and politicians in the participating countries. The method should increase the effectiveness of the national, regional and local administrations in focusing existing resources on priorities in order to accelerate the rehabilitation process of as many endangered monuments as possible. It should also facilitate the contacts and negotiation with potential donors or investors in providing detailed studies, a comprehensible methodology and an understanding of prioritisation, corresponding to the essential questions raised in a market economy looking for the best possible use of limited resources.

Latin School, Cincu, Romania

5.0 Example of a Heritage Assessment, Prioritised Intervention List and Preliminary Technical Assessment

The example given here, completed as part of the Integrated Rehabiliation Project Plan / Survey of the Architectural and Archaeological Heritage (Regional Programme for Cultural and Natural Heritage in South East Europe) in 2003, 2004 and 2005, was published by the Council of Europe.It is taken from one country, Montenegro (Serbia and Montenegro) and uses one building as an example, in order to demonstrate the continuity of the process.

5.1 Example of a Heritage Assessment

Heritage Assessment for Montenegro (Serbia and Montenegro)

Foreword

This Report on the architectural and archaeological heritage in Montenegro gives a general description of the situation pertaining in 2003. It contributes to the understanding of the legal and administrative mechanisms for managing the protection, the conservation and the enhancement of the heritage as well as its main features. It highlights the potential and the weaknesses to be taken into account when considering the elaboration of integrated rehabilitation projects. The Report was prepared by Mr Daniel Drocourt (France) in co-ordination and consultation with Ms Lidija Ljesar, IRPP/SAAH Project Co-ordinator. It was prepared following the receipt of responses to the initial questionnaire and a visit to the country by Mr Drocourt, during which wide consultations took place. The text presented here is an edited version of the original published account.

The published report is accompanied by a full Prioritised Intervention List of ten monuments and sites, compiled by the Project Co-ordinator. This identifies the historic buildings and sites that are of particular significance to the European heritage and urgently require conservation and/or restoration. It provides a snapshot of priorities from a specific standpoint and is by definition provisional, reflecting a consensus of local, regional and national views at a particular moment in time. It encompasses all the physical (natural and man-made), sociological, economic, cultural, ethnic and religious elements of the heritage. One example, the Kosmac Fortress, has been taken from this list and is published here as Example 5.2.

Introduction

The Republic of Montenegro possesses a rich architectural and archaeo-logical heritage, and different cultures have left behind traces of their exis-tence there. The most ancient evidence of human occupation dates back to the prehistoric period. Located in a territory that straddles the two worlds of East and West, the Montenegrin heritage is imbued with very diverse cultural and artistic influences – Byzantine, Islamic, Venetian and Austro-Hungarian.

However, this rich Montenegrin heritage (both movable and immovable) is in imminent danger. First of all, uncontrolled urbanisation is threatening rural and environmental ensembles. Some sacred monuments that have been permanently damaged by unskilled conservation are also endan-gered. However, the movable property belonging to sacred and secular monuments (paintings, icons, books) is facing an even greater threat.

Heritage

The most important buildings belonging to the immovable heritage are in the Class 1 Cultural Monuments category, which includes the most valu-able monuments of Montenegro's cultural heritage. The most important building ensembles are monumental and urban. The main archaeological sites are Crvena Stjena (Red Rock) near Niksic, Duklja (the ancient city of Doclea) in Podgorica, Municipium near Pljevlja and Risinium (Risan). The main architectural ensembles are urban ensembles and the ancient towns of Kotor, Cetinje, Budva, Ulcinj, Bar and Herceg-Novi. These ensembles contain the largest number of individual cultural monuments.

Priority should be given to the establishment of a new inventory of cul-tural monuments and the creation of an appropriate database. At the same time, particular attention should be paid at the management level to sacred monuments which are the victims of a poor conservation and restoration policy.

The main weakness in the Republic of Montenegro with regard to her-itage management is the lack of integrated protection for the built her-itage, cultural landscapes and natural environment. One of the sites that typify the current situation with regard to protection is the town of Kotor, where it is essential to consider the character of the heritage and the nat-ural and cultural aspects which caused the town to be placed on the UNESCO World Heritage List. In order to achieve the integrated protec-tion of the heritage, it is recommended that a specialist agency should be established, managed by a curator, capable of directing a specialised con-struction unit.

The renovation of historic buildings is mainly funded from the budget of the Montenegrin Ministry of Culture. The institutions responsible for the protection of the built heritage play a very important role in channelling the funds allocated by the Ministry of Culture in this area. Control of the financial resources is the same for both national and international funding. In certain cases, funding controls are more complex (eg. obligation to announce the public funding process on the website).

The restoration of a private building is usually funded by the owner of the property.

The relationships between institutions for the protection of the built heritage and urban planning are generally indirect. They are established through municipal agencies, which is inconvenient because these agencies have few skills in the heritage field. In the last few years, instances of failure to respect legal procedures have been recorded in the case of reconstruction work on cultural monuments. There is a palpable lack of professional documentation and of expert monitoring by the institutions responsible in this area. Although the basic conditions for protection exist, some examples show that there is a lack of consistency in implementing the regulations.

Legislation

The law currently in force in the Republic of Montenegro is the Law on the Protection of Cultural Monuments of 1991. A revision process aimed at drafting a new law is currently under way and should be completed in 2004. Local experts are supporting this process by making recommendations, and it is also planned to involve international experts.

The current law contains specific definitions on the protection of cultural monuments: what constitutes a cultural monument; the criteria according to which a monument may be designated as cultural; and describes ways of assessing monuments according to categories of importance, etc.

According to the current Law, if a monument is to be designated a cultural monument, it must incorporate various values – archaeological, artistic, historic, ethnological, architectural, urban, social, technical – that are important for the history and culture of Montenegro. Depending on their importance, cultural monuments in Montenegro are divided into three categories:

– major cultural monuments

– very important cultural monuments

– important cultural monuments

Management

Two institutes are responsible for the protection of the built heritage:
- The Republic Institute for Protection of Cultural Monuments, in Cetinje
- The Regional Institute for Protection of Cultural Monuments, in Kotor

There is also a Montenegro Centre for Archaeological Research, which is based in Podgorica.

Responsibility for looking after sacred monuments, which comprise 60% of the total of protected monuments, lies with the national institutions concerned with protection, in accordance with the Law on the Protection of Cultural Monuments.

The Minister for Culture is responsible for the overall supervision of the work of the Agency for the Protection of Cultural Monuments, while the specialised institutions, the Republic and Regional Institutes for the Protection of Cultural Monuments, supervise the professional work relating to the protection of the built heritage. Co-operation between these two Institutes is very good. In the municipalities, there are offices for cultural affairs, urban planning and the protection of the cultural and natural heritage.

The institutions responsible for the protection of the built heritage have short-term plans and programmes, but there is no specific management system nor a strategic plan for the future management of the built heritage overall.

With regard to the urban planning process and the construction of new buildings, there is a clear lack of synchronisation and co-ordination between the players involved, which is often to the detriment of cultural monuments and the built heritage.

Professional competence of the staff within the national institutions is satisfactory, but there is a lack of people with certain specialised skills in specific fields (architects, archaeologists, art historians).

The official institutes and organisations that play a role in the protection of the historic heritage, are involved with various exhibitions and publications and provide the public with definitions of historic buildings, thereby participating indirectly in the educational process.

The importance of the cultural heritage may be demonstrated in an accessible manner through various media, radio, the internet, people's forums and other forms of publicity. Schoolchildren can be educated though the primary and secondary curricula by studying subjects relevant to the cultural heritage, noting its importance and the need to preserve it. Advice and recommendations from international organisations with similar experience would be welcomed.

Partnerships

The most common form of heritage co-operation is with the institutions responsible for the built heritage, especially the museums, archives and universities.

There are also regular contacts and joint activities conducted by the Institute for the Protection of Cultural Monuments with such partner organisations as museums and archives. This is reflected very well in the joint promotion of the cultural heritage through exhibitions and publications. For many years, students, structural engineers and, in particular, architects have been able to find temporary employment or work experience arising from partnership activities.

Collaborative projects with other partners in the field of the built heritage are frequently carried out. The Regional Institute for the Protection of Cultural Monuments is working on cleaning the Kotor Fortress in co-operation with the Employment Bureau and the Kotor Local Town Planning Office. Similar projects for the fortresses of Herceg Novi are also about to be launched.

As far as international partnerships are concerned, mechanisms for discussing, approving and assessing proposed works were established after the 1979 earthquake. These mechanisms take the form of missions organised by the UNESCO agencies (ICCROM, ICOMOS) and student camps. After a long break, this co-operation is being renewed.

Funding by international organisations has recently been used for the implementation of the UNESCO Programme of Participation for 2002-2003, which involved the funding of studies and the revitalisation of the Kotor Fortress, and with a project supported by the American Embassy in Serbia and Montenegro to renovate part of the fortress.

There are also several projects in the pipeline, such as the equipping of the architectural workshop and construction unit of the Regional Institute for the Protection of Cultural Monuments, the Cultural Grassroots of Japan project and two partner projects with the UNIADRON organisation and the University of Bologna (education in the conservation and renovation of the Kotor Fortress).

Documentation

The Institute for the Protection of Cultural Monuments and the Centre for Archaeological Research are responsible for documentation.

There is a national inventory, which is incorporated into the Central Registry in the Institute in Cetinje. It essentially contains the basic characteristics of all monuments recorded in the Central Register and also includes ensembles. The inventory is currently being revised: some adjustments are necessary in order to bring it into line with European standards. The documentation is not in electronic form and there is no clear classification of the ensembles protected in the land registry.

Virtually all the documentation is available for public consultation, but the information is neither indexed nor retrievable electronically. It is however generally possible to access planning information. It is also possible to draw upon the expertise which is necessary for the prioritisation of buildings and sites. The institutions responsible for the protection of the built heritage possess adequate photographic equipment.

As far as staff trained in documentation are concerned, there are professionals in the national institutions. But, there is little expertise at the local level and it could be supplemented by means of a national initiative. There are experts in particular building types who can be called upon to assist. At the same time, representatives of different ethnic communities can be involved in the programme. Structural expertise is available to enable damage and repair costs to be assessed.

Ethnicity and community

Several national communities co-exist In Montenegro: Bosnian Muslims, Albanians, Croats and Roma. There is a governmental representative for national minorities: the Republic of Montenegro Ministry for the Protection of Minority Rights. Several NGOs operate in the country, their main purpose being the presentation and promotion of the culture and cultural heritage of the Bosnian Muslims. The Croat community also has its own NGOs and cultural associations, which actively co-operate with the state institutions.

Sources

Ministry of Culture in the Republic of Montenegro

Republic Institute for Protection of Cultural Monuments, Cetinje

Regional Institute for Protection of Cultural Monuments, Kotor

Centre for Archaeological Research of Montenegro

Published sources

Cultural monuments of Montenegro, Ministry of Culture, 1997

Information about condition of immovable cultural monuments of Montenegro, Ministry of Culture, 2001

Documentation Centre material:

– Republic Institute for Protection of Cultural Monuments, Cetinje

– Regional Institute for Protection of Cultural Monuments, Kotor

– Centre for archaeological research of Montenegro

Prioritised Intervention List

Summary

The Prioritised Intervention List of Montenegro comprises 10 monuments, ensembles and sites:

1. Duklja-Doclea – Ancient Roman town, Podgorica
2. Remains of the Ancient Roman Villa – Rizinium, Risan, Kotor
3. Fortifications of Kotor
4. Old Town of Bar
5. Hussein-Pasha Mosque, Pljevlja
6. Zabljak of Crnojevici, urban ensemble, Skadar Lake, Cetinje
7. Church of St. Eustahija, Dobrota, Kotor
8. Church of St. Nikola, Nikoljac, Bijelo Polje
9. Building of the French Embassy, Cetinje
10. Kosmac Fortress, Brajici, Budva

The list includes:

2 archaeological sites

2 fortifications

2 churches

1 mosque

2 urban ensembles

1 secular building

The significance of these has been assessed as follows:

Universal value (1)

International importance (4)

Special national importance (4)

Regional importance (1)

1 of these has had preliminary costings.

The majority of the sites and buildings have been assessed as high priority for intervention (7) with the remainder of medium priority.

It is believed that this selection of monuments, selected for further technical assessment and costings, offers a range of buildings and sites, representative of the rich heritage of Montenegro.

5.2 Example of a PIL entry

Kosmac fortress

Country or territory:

MONTENEGRO

Name of organisation compiling the information:

Ministry of Culture

Contact name:

Lidija Ljesar

Email address:

min.kulture.rcg@cg.yu

Name and address of building(s) or site:

KOSMAC FORTRESS, Brajici, Budva

Inventory reference number(s):

Decree No. 08-1027, 22nd August 1964

Building type(s):

Architectural monument; Fortification

Main date(s):

Middle of the 19th century

Current use(s):

No functional use

Significance:

The Austrian fortress Kosmac was constructed over a period of ten years. The construction probably began after the official establishment of the border between Montenegro and Austria in 1841 and ended approximately in 1850. During the 1st World War, the fortress was of service to the Austrians. In the 2nd World War, it was used by Italian soldiers. After the end of the war, the fort was abandoned, its condition deteriorated and the roof and the upper storey collapsed. The fortification is built of finely dressed grey limestone from the local quarries. It consists of a ground floor, upper storey and a spacious basement. The facades are segmented by rectangular windows and arched openings for gun barrels. The garrison building, no longer existing, was built near the fortress. A cistern between the two constructions remains.

Category of significance:

Of international importance

Category of ownership or interest:

Characteristic example of Austrian fortification.

Documentation and bibliographic references:

Documentation

– Inclusion in the Central Registry of Protected Cultural Monuments of Montenegro.

Bibliography

1. Luketic, M., *Budva*, Cetinje, 1966.
2. Markovic, C., and Vujicic, R., *Spomonici Kulture Crne Gore,* Novi Sad, 1997.

Condition:

Category 1, Very bad

Risk:

Risk depends on natural deterioration factors since the building is not adequately protected. The fortress is also at risk of being vandalised. There is also risk related to the management of the site.

Condition risk:

Category A, Immediate risk of further rapid deterioration or loss of fabric; no solution agreed.

Technical assessment and costing:

None carried out.

Ownership:

The Republic Institute for Protection of Cultural Monuments

Occupation:

Unoccupied; not in use

Management:

Management by the state

Summary:

The Kosmac Fortress is a characteristic example of Austrian fortification. It is not adequately protected and so is at risk through natural deterioration, vandalism and inadequate site management.

The Fortress Kosmac has a high level of potential priority.

Sign. and date

Lidija Ljesar

February 2004

5.3 Example of a PTA entry

Fortress Kosmac

1. Introductory page

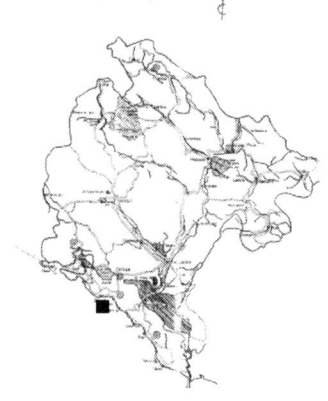

Site map   The Kosmač Fortress

1.1 Country or Territory:

Republic of Montenegro

1.2 Name of organisation compiling the information:

Ministry of Culture and Media of Montenegro

1.3 Contact name:

Lidija Ljesar

1.4 Email address:

min.kulture.rcg@cg.yu

1.5 Name and address of building or site:

Fortress Kosmač, Brajici, Budva

1.6 Inventory reference number(s):

Decree No. 08-1027 from 22 August 1964, Central Registry of Cultural Monuments of Montenegro

1.7 Building/Monument/Site type:

Architectural monument, military architecture, fortification

1.8 Main dates:

1841 – 1850

1.9 Current use(s):

None

2. Executive Summary: the site and its management

Fortress Kosmac is situated on a hilltop adjacent to the village of Brajici, near Budva, at a height of 800m above sea level. It was built between 1841-1850 by the Austrians at the border between Montenegro and Austria.

The entire fortification is built of finely dressed grey limestone from local quarries. Its ground plan is irregular and elongated, with two wings separated by a large circular tower. The fort consists of ground floor, upper storey and a large basement, in all around 1064 square metres. Nothing now remains of a garrison building of more recent date which was located adjacent to the fortress. In the spacious courtyard, there was a cistern.

Kosmac is the key fortification in the area, forming the final defensive position in the chain of fortresses that defined the border. It is a typical example of the Austro- Hungarian fortified architecture of that time in the area of the south-cast Adriatic coast. The construction techniques used were well developed and the fortress represents a striking achievement of military architecture of that period.

Because of the specific climatic conditions – the combination of mountain and littoral climate – this is an important spa area.

The fortress is in a highly dilapidated condition. It has lost its roof structure, significant parts of its internal structural walling and floors, and is at risk of continued collapse. Its significance lies primarily in being one of a series of similar monuments and its conservation should preserve this spirit and the form that the building presents. Other fortresses of the group probably have more architectural or historical significance, and they also have undergone certain conservation works through being part of urban settings. Kosmac has been unjustifiably neglected over decades: its accessibility and outstanding location make it potentially more attractive for investment for some tourist or commercial use then other fortifications.

It offers the opportunity for either modest consolidation, the preservation of a ruin, or more substantial reconstruction perhaps to a commercial use. Its location close to the tourist centre of Budva and the coast offers this potential.

The primary purpose of this proposal is to bring this important monument back into some sustainable and appropriate use and protect it from irreversible deterioration. It can be saved, but only through immediate intervention. The current proposals are to convert the building into an hotel or hostel, such as self-catering holiday apartments or youth hostel accommodation, or as a complex with a cultural function for the various activities and needs of the Republic Institute: seminars, workshops, exhibitions, specialised summer schools etc. Alternatively it could be preserved as a ruin and site of memory.

The key issue is whether the building can be sensitively adapted to a new use without losing its essential architectural characteristics, and this must form the subject of a further feasibility study.

3. Administrative information

3.1 Responsible Authorities

Kosmač is owned by the Republic Institute for Protection of Cultural Monuments of Montenegro.

Both local authorities of the Municipality of Budva and the Republic Institute for Protection of Cultural Monuments of Montenegro (State Institution) have statutory and managerial responsibility for the fortification.

3.2 Building/Site, Name and Address

Fortification Kosmač, hill Kosmač, Brajici village, Budva.

3.3 Map reference

x = 42° 18' E, y = 18° 57' N

3.4 Type of monument

Architectural monument, military architecture, fortification

3.5 Ownership

Republic Institute for Protection of Cultural Monuments of Montenegro.

3.6 Statutory Protection/Constraints

Fortification Kosmač is listed in the Central Registry as a cultural monument of category III, so it is subject to certain statutory constraints. The limitations on activities are included in the spatial and master planning of the territory of the Republic and local authorities. For all activities, prior conservation terms must be established and issued by the relevant authority, the Republic Institute for Protection of Cultural Monuments. Prior to any construction activity, a permit must be issued by the Ministry for Protection of Environment and Spatial Planning.

4. Summary of condition

4.1 Summary of Physical Condition

Very bad: the loss of the roof and progressive collapse of the external and internal walls is leading to collapse of the structure.

4.2 Condition Risk Assessment – graded A-H

B – Immediate risk of further rapid deterioration or loss of fabric; solution agreed but not begun

4.3 Priority for intervention – High/Medium/Low

High priority

5. Existing information

5.1 Documentary sources:

Most of the documents related to the fortress can be found in the Republic Institute for the Protection of Cultural Monuments:

- Dossier of the Monument according to the Law on Protection of Cultural Monuments, 1991
- Report on Condition with photographic documentation of the Fortress Kosmač, by Commission for Assessment of Immovable Cultural Heritage in Montenegro, July 2004.
- Report on Condition with photographic documentation, Republic Institute for the Protection of Cultural Monuments, 1997, Cetinje

5.2 Bibliography:

1. Luketic, M., *Budva*, Cetinje, 1966.

2. Markovic, C., and Vujicic, R., *Spomonici Kulture Crne Gore*, Novi Sad, 1997.

5.3 Fieldwork already conducted:

While compiling the Report on the Condition of the Fortress Kosmač in July 2004, a general technical assessment was carried out. Recommendations: creation of the conservation project and adequate presentation of the site.

5.4 Projects in progress:

None

5.5 Projects already planned:

None

5.6 Financial estimates already made:

None

6. Scope of the PTA

6.1 Extent/Nature of the assessment:

The following were involved in the preparation of the PTA:

David Johnson – Conservation Architect, London, UK

Emma Carmichael – Conservation Building Surveyor, London, UK

Lidija Ljesar – Conservator/Restorer, Ministry of Culture and Media of Montenegro, Podgorica

Zorana Milosevic – Conservation Architect, Regional Institute for the Protection of Cultural Monuments, Kotor

Tanja Vujovic – Ethnologist/Conservator, Republic Institute for the Protection of Cultural Monuments, Cetinje

Aleksandra Kapetanovic, Conservation Architect, NGO EXPEDITIO, Kotor

6.2 Limitations of the study:

1. Physical structure of the building – large quantity of fallen masonry around and inside the building prevent real examination of the structure.
2. Loss of the vertical communication inside the building prevent access to the upper storeys.
3. Site does not have necessary infrastructure, such as electricity.

Situation on 29th November 2004, field work:

The Fortress is in very poor condition, and much of it is obscured by fallen masonry which prevented a thorough examination of the entire structure and fabric. Access was only available up to 2 metres above ground. No access was available to the upper floor levels which are deteriorating seriously due to the loss of the roof. No lighting was available internally, the inspection having to be carried out in natural lighting conditions which were poor due to the very foggy conditions in which the survey was carried out.

7. The PTA

7.1 Background

7.1.1 Summary description of the building/site

The Fortress is symmetrical in plan and originally 3 stories high. It is assumed that the last construction above the third storey was covered by concrete plate which has fully collapsed. This assumption was based on examples of other Austrian fortifications on the Montenegrin coast. The walls are stone built. There are 2 semicircular wings facing east at the ends of the central section of the building. A further semicircular wing in the centre of the building containing what appears to have been a staircase, now collapsed, faces west and seaward. The plan of the building breaks along its centreline at an angle of around 20°, giving the fortress views in 8 directions as well as the views from the semicircular wings.

The building is located at the summit of a steep hill overlooking the town of Budva on a site of around 3500 square metres.

7.1.2 Summary historic development and evolution of the building or site, from the earliest times until the present day.

It took some ten years to construct the Austrian fortress Kosmac: begun probably after the official establishment of borders between Montenegro and Austria (1841), the works were finished about 1850.

The Austrian Emperor Franz Joseph visited the fortress in 1875. The fortress served the Austrians during the Great War, and in the 2nd World War it was an Italian outpost until their capitulation in 1943. After the latter war had ended, the fort was abandoned and parts of it have now crumbled. It is now roofless and without an upper storey.

7.2 Significance

7.2.1 Summary statement of significance/historical and heritage importance.

The fortress was built in the period of Austrian occupation as the key fortified building in this area. It is a very important building historically because it was the final point in the chain of fortresses that defined the border between Montenegro and Austria.

The location which was chosen for constructing this fortress together with the fortress itself is very prominent and dominates the Riviera of Budva, and it is very significant from the symbolic point of view as well as the landscape.

It is a typical example of Austro-Hungarian fortified architecture of the time in the area of the south-east Adriatic coast. Construction techniques are at a high level and it may be considered a very good achievement of the military architecture of that period.

Because of the specific climate conditions, a combination of mountain and littoral climate, this location is an important spa area.

Evaluation of the significance:

7.2.2 Historical

high

7.2.3 Artistic/Aesthetic

medium

7.2.4 Technological

medium

7.2.5 Religious/Spiritual

low

7.2.6 Symbolic/Identity

high

7.2.7 Scientific/Research

medium

7.2.8 Social/Civic

7.2.9 Natural

medium

7.2.10 Economic

low

7.2.11 Category of significance:

International – East Adriatic Coast.

7.3 Vulnerability/Risk assessment.

7.3.1. Natural threats:

The roof of the fortress has been destroyed and the internal fabric is therefore completely exposed to the weather. One section of the second floor construction has collapsed. Further collapse is inevitable.

7.3.2. Looting:

The theft of external facing stones has undermined the external walling in several places and the walls are progressively collapsing.

The structure is dangerous, which is a serious risk to the public who can freely enter the site.

7.3.3. Development threats:

The fortress is located in the hills above the town of Budva, not far from the main road between Budva and Podgorica. It is therefore in an area of potential development, and has already experienced a certain amount of building development on the slopes immediately below the fortress. Continued expansion constitutes an on-going threat to the setting.

7.3.4. Maintenance

There is currently no maintenance of the building or its infrastructure to arrest the continued decay.

There is no project of priority protection for the Fortress.

The fortress does not have a function at present.

7.3.5. Resources

The principle cause of failure and deterioration of the fabric has been the lack of available finances for maintenance and repair.

7.4 Technical condition and 7.5 Outline summary of required repairs

The building is in a dilapidated condition, the roof having completely collapsed, and the remaining walls and floors are in various states of collapse.

Internal condition

Floor and ceiling:

Condition:

The ground floor is completely covered by a large amount of rubble which has collapsed from the structure. The upper floor structures are stone vaulted suggesting that the floor finishes may well have been stone, but further investigation is required to confirm the real condition. The south bay of the first floor in the main north-south chamber is the only part of this floor remaining. In the north wing the first floor structures have collapsed. In the south wing the first floor structures remain, but have started to collapse.

Repairs:

The existing rubble needs removing, selecting and storing for reuse. The floors will need to be comprehensively reconstructed to prevent further collapse.

Walls:

Condition:

A significant number of the internal structural walls have partially collapsed, particularly the wall between the main chamber of the fortress and the north tower. The wall has been reduced to a single skin at this position. There is some evidence of some walls having originally been plastered.

Repairs:

Major repairs are required to the walling, first to consolidate and make safe and then more comprehensively if a new use is to be found.

External condition

Roofs:

Condition:

The roofs of the building have been completely destroyed and there is no site evidence of the original construction. It is assumed that the last construction above the third storey was stone vaulted covered by concrete plate which fully collapsed.

Repairs:

– It might be possible to consolidate the existing walls and floor structures and preserve the fortress as a ruin, with no roof interventions being envisaged;

– Alternatively, the roofs could be rebuilt to allow the building to be re-used.

– Partial restoration would be a further option.

Reconstruction would need to be carried out on the basis of surviving documentary records of the construction and of information *in situ.*

Walls:

Condition:

The walls appear to be of traditional stone masonry with internal and finely dressed external leaves of ashlar walling and stone rubble infill. Looting of the lower levels of the external ashlar has led to progressive collapse of the external facing. There are also serious structural cracks throughout the walling resulting from the gradual loss of internal floors and the roof.

Repairs:

The walls require extensive rebuilding to arrest continued deterioration.

Site:

Condition:

The fortress sits on a confined level site which has been partially cleared of the remains of outbuildings, although there are substantial amounts of masonry littered across the site. The building is approached along a narrow rubble road which is negotiable by vehicles, although deeply rutted. There is a second track leading from the summit which rejoins the main track part way down the hill.

Repairs:

The site should be generally consolidated and made safe; the extent of repairs depend on the final use of the fortress.

7.6 Conservation policy and proposals

7.6.1

Kosmač Fortress is one in a group of similar Austrian built fortifications lining the coastal fringe of Montenegro. It commands an impressive location high above the town of Budva and can be seen from a wide area.

Other fortresses of the group probably have more architectural or historical significance, and they also underwent certain conservation works since they are part of urban settings. On the other hand, Kosmac was unjustifiably neglected over decades, which led to a very high level of structural deterioration, while the accessibility and outstanding location of Kosmač make it potentially more attractive for investment for some tourist or commercial use then other fortifications.

The fortress will remain in the ownership of the Institute for the Protection of Cultural Monuments, but a lease could be granted to a suitable organisation if an adequate use can be found.

7.6.2 Conservation philosophy

The principle to be followed is to preserve as much as possible of the original building and its materials: those materials which remain in the Fortress appear to be wholly original. The fabric is of stone construction throughout and the plan form does not seem to have been modified. The loss of the entire roof of the building, however, has effectively removed any possibility of consolidation of the building by any method other than reconstruction, unless it is proposed to retain the fortress in the long term as a ruin.

The repairs required are very extensive and will require high investment which in turn may demand the type of use which will attract a commercial sponsor.

7.6.3 Level of intervention

The preliminary intention for the conservation of the fortress is to restore the physical appearance of the building as far as possible while recognising that a new use may demand some alteration of certain parts of the exterior. The form of the building should not however be altered. The building is very clearly a fortification, and this quality should not be compromised.

Internally, the form of the building should again be respected, although apart from the main structural elements the interior has been so severely damaged that unless clear evidence of its original planning and detail can be found through historical research, the internal layout is open to speculation.

The building has been so severely damaged that at least partial reconstruction will be necessary to bring the building back into habitable use. The building could be conserved as a ruin, but the amount of work required to do this might not be justifiable.

7.6.4 Preliminary proposals for appropriate uses

Alternative uses being considered are: commercial use for the purpose of tourism (such as transit tourism) or hostel (such as self catering holiday apartments or youth hostel accommodation) or a site with a cultural function for the different activities and needs (seminars, workshops, exhibitions, specialised summer schools) of the Republic Institute; site of memory and preservation as a ruin.

7.6.5 Opportunities for social uses and sustainable development

The location and accessibility of the fortress offer great potential for sustainable development for tourist use. Revitalisation of this building for the purposes proposed in paragraph 7.6.4 would open many opportunities for social use and sustainable development, such as the creation of work places, engagement in social services, other activities such as tourism, information, museum activities, seminars, workshops, etc.

7.6.6 Broad assessment of priorities for consolidation/covering, repair, conservation, restoration, rehabilitation

The basic priorities for the consolidation of the fortress are to prevent further deterioration. This will require:

- removing, selecting and storing of the material;
- research and architectural survey;
- project design;
- extensive rebuilding of the structure both inside and out which will need to be assessed in consultation with a structural engineer. In parallel, the exposed second floor of the building will need to be protected.

If an alternative use can be established which requires the reconstruction of the building, this should be completed as a single phase of work. Ideally the fitting out of the building should be completed as part of this phase.

7.6.7 Public access

Public access is currently freely available to the site, and if the building is consolidated as a ruin this will remain its primary use. In any new use, public access should be retained and coordinated with that use.

7.6.8 Other benefits

Organised visits aiming at presentation of cultural heritage monuments; performing arts events; certain types of sports, recreational activities; spas, etc.

7.7 Finance

7.7.1 Broad assessment of budgetary needs and phasing

Alternative 1: consolidation – total (€)	**1,148,800.00**
Preparatory works – total:	**38,000.00**
– enabling contract to clear building and site	15,500.00
– measured survey	4,500.00
– structural survey	4,500.00
– project design	13,500.00
Building works – total	**708,750.00**
– preparation of the building site	67,500.00
– demolition of existing structures	67,500.00
– consolidation and reconstruction of walls and foundations	135,000.00
– new building constructions	236,250.00
– repairs to roof	101,250.00
– repairs to internal walls and floors	67,500.00
– fitting out	33,750.00
New services installations – total	**236,250.00**
– electric installations (lighting, heating, telecommunications, etc)	168,750.00
– water and sewage installations	67,500.00
Other costs – total	**165,800.00**
– Consultants fees	67,500.00
– contingency	98,300.00

Alternative 2: reconstruction - total (€)	**1,705,200.00**
Preparatory works – total	**47,000.00**
– enabling contract to clear building and site	15,500.00
– measured survey	4,500.00
– structural survey	6,500.00
– project design	20,500.00
Building works – total	**1,104,200.00**
– preparation of the building site	90,500.00
– demolition of existing structures	67,500.00
– consolidation and reconstruction of walls and foundations	135,000.00
– new building constructions	472,500.00
– repairs to roof	202,500.00
– repairs to internal walls and floors	90,500.00
– fitting out	45,700.00
New services installations – total	**316,700.00**
– electric installations (lighting, heating, telecommunications, etc)	226,200.00
– water and sewage installations	90,500.00
Other costs – total	**237,300.00**
– Consultants fees	90,500.00
– contingency	146,800.00

7.7.2 Assessment of possibilities for attracting investments.

Official assessment of possibilities for attracting investments has not been done so far. However, having in mind the above mentioned future uses, we believe they could attract investment, taking into consideration other sources of financing, donations, grants, co-financing, tax policies, etc.

7.7.3 Assessment of possibilities for recovering investments

Official assessment of possibilities for recovering investments has not been done so far, but we believe that the investment will be returned through services, working places, etc.

7.7.4 Have you already tried to raise funds for this site or monument? If so, provide details.

Never

7.7.5 Have you already received funds for this site or monument? If so, provide details.

Never

7.8 Management

7.8.1 The Republic of Montenegro through the responsible Ministry of Culture carries out supervision in terms of respecting legal regulations for the protection of cultural monuments. Specialised institutions are dealing with the protection policy and its monitoring: the Republic and Regional Institutes for the Protection of Cultural Monuments. The ultimate aim of the protection of cultural monuments is for them to have a purpose, and to enable the user of the individual object to carry out constant management.

7.8.2 The Republic of Montenegro is dedicated to the protection of its cultural and historic heritage fulfilling this activity as an activity of special social interest. In 1964, the fortress Kosmač was listed in the Central Registry of protected cultural monuments, and since then it has occasionally been the subject of professional and scientific considerations. The legal position with respect to the ownership of this complex is clear and defined, which should make any activity on the fort less complicated. The Law defines the obligations of all concerned in the domain of protection of cultural monuments, as well as the responsibilities of national institutions for the protection of the heritage, which should guarantee the safety of future investments.

8. Supporting Documentation

CD with 9 photographs

Drawings

Plan

Section from the military map

9. Feasibility Studies

The proposals for the re-use of Kosmac Fortress vary from its preservation and consolidation as a ruin, through to reconstruction with a modern commercial function such as use as a hotel or hostel. An architect and a structural engineer will be required for the next phase of assessment.

Even as a preserved ruin, a significant element of structural repair will be required, and a structural survey with recommendations should be produced. This will require the removal and storage, where appropriate, of material and the provision of safe access to the building.

Several other elements should be reviewed at the outset of the feasibility stage which could fundamentally affect the future use:

Services

Utility services will be required on the site, particularly if an hotel use is considered. Power, water, drainage and data supplies will all need to be provided and this could have a major cost impact upon the proposals. There may also be archaeological implications.

Research

Proposals for reconstruction of the building will need to be carried out on the basis of surviving documentary records of the construction and of information *in situ*. The level and detail of the information available could significantly affect the use of the building. An archaeological desk study should be prepared, with recommendations for site investigations.

Access

A new or improved access road will be required, its extent and scale being dependent upon the proposed use. This could have planning and ownership implications.

Design proposals

Sketch design proposals should be prepared for the various options. A measured survey of the existing buildings should be completed in advance to assist with this process.

PTA carried out by:

PTA Local Experts Working Group

Ms Lidija Ljesar, Project Coordinator for Montenegro

Podgorica, 31 January 2005.

Sales agents for publications of the Council of Europe
Agents de vente des publications du Conseil de l'Europe

BELGIUM/BELGIQUE
La Librairie européenne SA
50, avenue A. Jonnart
B-1200 BRUXELLES 20
Tel.: (32) 2 734 0281
Fax: (32) 2 735 0860
E-mail: info@libeurop.be
http://www.libeurop.be

Jean de Lannoy
202, avenue du Roi
B-1190 BRUXELLES
Tel.: (32) 2 538 4308
Fax: (32) 2 538 0841
E-mail: jean.de.lannoy@euronet.be
http://www.jean-de-lannoy.be

CANADA
Renouf Publishing Company Limited
5369 Chemin Canotek Road
CDN-OTTAWA, Ontario, K1J 9J3
Tel.: (1) 613 745 2665
Fax: (1) 613 745 7660
E-mail: order.dept@renoufbooks.com
http://www.renoufbooks.com

CZECH REPUBLIC/
RÉPUBLIQUE TCHÈQUE
Suweco Cz Dovoz Tisku Praha
Ceskomoravska 21
CZ-18021 PRAHA 9
Tel.: (420) 2 660 35 364
Fax: (420) 2 683 30 42
E-mail: import@suweco.cz

DENMARK/DANEMARK
GAD Direct
Fiolstaede 31-33
DK-1171 COPENHAGEN K
Tel.: (45) 33 13 72 33
Fax: (45) 33 12 54 94
E-mail: info@gaddirect.dk

FINLAND/FINLANDE
Akateeminen Kirjakauppa
Keskuskatu 1, PO Box 218
FIN-00381 HELSINKI
Tel.: (358) 9 121 41
Fax: (358) 9 121 4450
E-mail: akatilaus@stockmann.fi
http://www.akatilaus.akateeminen.com

FRANCE
La Documentation française
(Diffusion/Vente France entière)
124, rue H. Barbusse
F-93308 AUBERVILLIERS Cedex
Tel.: (33) 01 40 15 70 00
Fax: (33) 01 40 15 68 00
E-mail: commandes.vel@ladocfrancaise.gouv.fr
http://www.ladocfrancaise.gouv.fr

Librairie Kléber (Vente Strasbourg)
Palais de l'Europe
F-67075 STRASBOURG Cedex
Fax: (33) 03 88 52 91 21
E-mail: librairie.kleber@coe.int

GERMANY/ALLEMAGNE
AUSTRIA/AUTRICHE
August Bebel Allee 6
Am Hofgarten 10
D-53175 BONN
Tel.: (49) 2 28 94 90 20
Fax: (49) 2 28 94 90 222
E-mail: bestellung@uno-verlag.de
http://www.uno-verlag.de

GREECE/GRÈCE
Librairie Kauffmann
28, rue Stadiou
GR-ATHINAI 10564
Tel.: (30) 1 32 22 160
Fax: (30) 1 32 30 320
E-mail: ord@otenet.gr

HUNGARY/HONGRIE
Euro Info Service
Hungexpo Europa Kozpont ter 1
H-1101 BUDAPEST
Tel.: (361) 264 8270
Fax: (361) 264 8271
E-mail: euroinfo@euroinfo.hu
http://www.euroinfo.hu

ITALY/ITALIE
Libreria Commissionaria Sansoni
Via Duca di Calabria 1/1, CP 552
I-50125 FIRENZE
Tel.: (39) 556 4831
Fax: (39) 556 41257
E-mail: licosa@licosa.com
http://www.licosa.com

NETHERLANDS/PAYS-BAS
De Lindeboom Internationale Publikaties
PO Box 202, MA de Ruyterstraat 20 A
NL-7480 AE HAAKSBERGEN
Tel.: (31) 53 574 0004
Fax: (31) 53 572 9296
E-mail: books@delindeboom.com
http://home-1-worldonline.nl/~lindeboo/

NORWAY/NORVÈGE
Akademika, A/S Universitetsbokhandel
PO Box 84, Blindern
N-0314 OSLO
Tel.: (47) 22 85 30 30
Fax: (47) 23 12 24 20

POLAND/POLOGNE
Głowna Księgarnia Naukowa
im. B. Prusa
Krakowskie Przedmiescie 7
PL-00-068 WARSZAWA
Tel.: (48) 29 22 66
Fax: (48) 22 26 64 49
E-mail: inter@internews.com.pl
http://www.internews.com.pl

PORTUGAL
Livraria Portugal
Rua do Carmo, 70
P-1200 LISBOA
Tel.: (351) 13 47 49 82
Fax: (351) 13 47 02 64
E-mail: liv.portugal@mail.telepac.pt

SPAIN/ESPAGNE
Mundi-Prensa Libros SA
Castelló 37
E-28001 MADRID
Tel.: (34) 914 36 37 00
Fax: (34) 915 75 39 98
E-mail: libreria@mundiprensa.es
http://www.mundiprensa.com

SWITZERLAND/SUISSE
Adeco – Van Diermen
Chemin du Lacuez 41
CH-1807 BLONAY
Tel.: (41) 21 943 26 73
Fax: (41) 21 943 36 05
E-mail: info@adeco.org

UNITED KINGDOM/ROYAUME-UNI
TSO (formerly HMSO)
51 Nine Elms Lane
GB-LONDON SW8 5DR
Tel.: (44) 207 873 8372
Fax: (44) 207 873 8200
E-mail: customer.services@theso.co.uk
http://www.the-stationery-office.co.uk
http://www.itsofficial.net

UNITED STATES and CANADA/
ÉTATS-UNIS et CANADA
Manhattan Publishing Company
2036 Albany Post Road
CROTON-ON-HUDSON,
NY 10520, USA
Tel.: (1) 914 271 5194
Fax: (1) 914 271 5856
E-mail: Info@manhattanpublishing.com
http://www.manhattanpublishing.com

Council of Europe Publishing/Editions du Conseil de l'Europe
F-67075 Strasbourg Cedex
Tel.: (33) 03 88 41 25 81 – Fax: (33) 03 88 41 39 10 – E-mail: publishing@coe.int – Website: http://book.coe.int